FUNDAMENTALS OF HR ANALYTICS

Fundamentals of HR Analytics *should be required reading for all HR Practitioners attempting to create value for their organisations, as well as to improve their own capabilities to gain insights in today's constantly changing world of work.*

'In God we trust, all others must bring data' is largely attributed to Deming and a good starting point for acknowledging that analytics has a place in all professional work. Past Examples of Six Sigma projects in HR have demonstrated the leverage this can provide in supporting organisational improvement. It is thus fitting that a more dedicated book be available to HR practitioners that takes into account the specific lexicon and context of the HR function, as well as the contemporary trends and technological advances available.

While this book is an important contribution to professionals regardless of their level of expertise, it is an equally powerful contribution to deepening the common understanding of effective HR practices. As HR functions support necessary business improvement processes, their own maturity of moving from Basic Personnel Administration through to People Development, Line Management Empowerment, Value Addition and finally Anticipating the Future, will also require an overlay in HR Analytics Maturity as described in this book.

— Dr Dino Petrarolo, SVP at Competitive Capabilities International and Best Practice Advisor

HR is at a major intersection whereby the future success of organizations will be reserved for those who are capable of best understanding people data and how such information can be leveraged to disrupt and grow. There is a continued need for HR leaders to understand business, not just people. This book dives in deep to what every high-performing HR leader needs to know about the incredible value than comes from a data-driven people-focused organization. Absorb what is in this book and deliver more value today by incorporating Fundamentals of HR Analytics *into your everyday work life!*

— Scott Cawood, President and CEO of WorldatWork, USA

What a great book! Business leaders look to HR for business solutions but are often disappointed. This book provides invaluable tools for HR practitioners to migrate from support to impactful business partners who deliver solutions that are bought into by senior leadership. I wholeheartedly recommend this book for all who are grappling with how to capitalise on the power offered by digital transformation and HR analytics to add greater value to their organisations. This book is written in an easy to understand format with many practical examples and case studies to illustrate the use of analytics to solve challenging problems that are commonplace in organisations.

— Mark Cotterrell, Chairman and CEO of MAC Consulting, South Africa

As a seasoned HR practitioner and academic, I found Fundamentals of HR Analytics *a worthwhile read. Whether you are just about to start your HR analytics journey or are wanting to secure HR's seat in the boardroom, this is a must-have and must-read book! The authors successfully present a comprehensive summary of the perplexing people analytics 'mystery', so I will surely be recommending this book to my students and colleagues.*

— Magda Bezuidenhout, PhD, Senior Lecturer in Compensation Management, University of South Africa

Arguably the biggest skill gap as the HR profession transforms in the digital age is in people analytics.

How can HR provide better visibility on an organisation's most important asset – its people. Where are the best opportunities to maximise ROI on human capital? Which events matter most to the employee experience? What predictive insights are possible to better enable workplace learning and agility? This book is therefore highly recommended as a must-read for both new and seasoned professionals. By enabling faster and better decisions, analytics will finally allow HR to re-claim its essence – to be more human.

— Mayank Parekh, Chief Executive Officer at the Institute for Human Resource Professionals, Singapore

It is an era of the Fourth Industrial Revolution and Big Data. It is fundamental that HR should remain relevant and aligned to the business objectives. This comprehensive analysis of HR drivers is essential and dynamic reading for all senior managers. It forms the basis for innovative decision-making and provides hands-on explanations with real-life case studies – from concept to implementation, in a context of global competition and added value for all stakeholders. Fundamentals of HR Analytics *should be required reading not only for HR professionals but also for senior managers.*

— James Allan, CEO of Sable Metals & Minerals, South Africa

Fundamentals of HR Analytics *is a must-read for any HR professional who wants to understand and apply data analytics to solve real HR challenges in organizations. This book offers practical guidance and demystifies analytics with clear step-by-step guidelines to develop data-driven, realistic and actionable solutions to the common problems around talent attraction, development, retention and engagement.*

— Aileen Tan, Group Chief HR Officer, SingTel, Singapore

FUNDAMENTALS OF HR ANALYTICS

A Manual on Becoming HR Analytical

FERMIN DIEZ
Singapore Management University, Singapore

MARK BUSSIN
21st Century Pay Solutions, South Africa

VENESSA LEE
United Overseas Bank, Singapore

United Kingdom – North America – Japan
India – Malaysia – China

Emerald Publishing Limited
Howard House, Wagon Lane, Bingley BD16 1WA, UK

First edition 2020

Reprints and permissions service
Contact: permissions@emeraldinsight.com

British Library Cataloguing in Publication Data
A catalogue record for this book is available from the British Library

ISBN: 978-1-78973-964-0 (Print)
ISBN: 978-1-78973-961-9 (Online)
ISBN: 978-1-78973-963-3 (Epub)

INVESTOR IN PEOPLE

TABLE OF CONTENTS

LIST OF FIGURES

FOREWORD

INFORMATION RICH, INSIGHT POOR. The digital transformation has been happening in HR for some time. With that
transformation has been a tremendous increase in the accessibility
of HR data. With so much data, HR professionals are faced with
how to consume these data. As a function we are not putting the
data to work for us to help us improve our organisation. This book,
written by Dr Fermin Diez, Dr Mark Bussin and Venessa Lee,
provides you the tools to make sense of all of this disparate information so you can make better HR business decisions.

I have had the pleasure to work with Fermin Diez in multiple
consultancies over the past 25 years. Both of us have been highly
aligned in terms of our passion for making better business decisions in the HR department through more fact-based analysis.
We have seen data accessibility with easier to use tools grow
exponentially and permitted us to work on projects that were
able to measure success of an HR program or how a particular
change in an HR program can deliver positive results for the
company. As for the overall HR function, the ways to analyse the
robust data sets have been left many times in the hands of consultants. This is changing. As HR strategies continue to better
align with the business strategy, the requirement for basic and
advanced HR analytics has increased. With the combination of
Fermin's, Mark's and Venessa's consulting background and
corporate experience, they bring a more practical approach to
HR analytics in this book which people can quickly adopt and
implement on their own.

In my 35 years of leading businesses that specialise in data,
technology and insights, I have seen the growing need for upgrading
the business acumen of the HR department (and even co-founded a
course of Business Acumen for the HR Professional through the

World@Work association). HR analytics is key to upgrading your business acumen. We see techniques that have been used on the sales side (from client acquisition factors to customer retention analysis) for a long time to apply these same techniques to the human capital of an organisation. By applying these techniques, you can improve the results of the organisation. Since human capital is usually the largest expense in your company, and since we really know the least about it, you can apply these techniques outlined in this book to make significant differences in your company. Huge opportunities exist in HR to gain advantages and insights by improving your company through HR analytics. Here are some first-hand experiences:

- Analytics identified how a high potential management program in a large manufacturing company was causing negative impacts to the company. The basis was that these high potential managers were moving on to the next roles too early and were not seeing their changes through completion. In other words, a high potential would get into a role, want to make changes to prove themselves, make the changes, but then started looking for their next role. This program was causing changes after changes in processes with no follow-through, which impacted productivity in a negative way.

- A large software company used analytics to provide a better measure on whether an expatriate assignment was determined to be successful based upon many factors. This company was growing in emerging markets and expatriation success was a key driver for their global success. Again, no one can measure someone's heart or mind, but based upon big data, a model could be developed on the probability of success for an expatriate move (as these moves are expensive!).

- Analytics determined that a company had the wrong balance of full-time and contingent workers. The company thought a strategy of having more cost-effective contingent workers was the right strategy. Unfortunately, the analytics highlighted how customer service degraded and impacted the company in a negative way. The analytics used were able to identify a more optimal balance of full-time employees and contingent workers.

These are just some of many types of analytics that utilise the tools that you will learn in the book and can apply them TODAY! As you read this book, remember the following:

1. **It's easy!**

   With so much information at your fingertips, there are excellent measures that can quickly be produced which can have immediate success in sharing with colleagues or the business. Many books in this area are highly technical and lack the practical nature of what is demonstrated in this book. In the past, the best word to describe data in HR was 'helter-skelter' because data were in different, completely unrelated systems. With digital transformation, many of these data sets are being brought together so that analysis can be performed on all of the data at one time as opposed to just pieces of the information. This provides easier and better analysis.

2. **The problem that you are trying to solve is your unique problem.**

   Context is everything. With HR analytics, this is not any different. You have a different business strategy than other companies, therefore, your HR strategy to achieve that business strategy is unique to your organisation. There is no prescribed answer to HR analytics. However, you can learn the tools and apply them to your specific circumstance and deliver the unique solution that will be best for your organisation.

3. **It's not about the data but the actionable insights.**

   This has been one of the major issues that HR professionals face: 'I have so much data, what do I do now?' As with any solution, you need to address a problem or hypothesis. Are there key success factors that relate to the HR strategy that will be used to implement the business strategy? Focus on those areas where there are clear issues for success. With this problem at hand, you begin the slow process of understanding what are the factors that impact the problems and make sure that you have data that can be used in various ways, as outlined in the book, to help measure, explain or address the issue.

The best insights are those that you can take an action to address. Yes, it is great to understand trends. However, it is better if you understand the trends, then take an action that will improve it and, most importantly, measure the improvement!

4. Predictive analytics and simulations are the best!

In HR analytics, you have different measures that have difference strengths in understanding of the impact. You first start with anecdotal data. You hear from someone that this one person has an issue and then many want to generalise that to everyone then having a similar issue. This is the weakest measure. Using turnover as an example, you always hear that this key staff person left the company because base salaries at our organisation are low. Is this the real reason why the person left? As we know, pay is an important element but there are many other factors that drive turnover.

Next type of measure, you have reality checks. This begins a more fact-based examination. You go to make sure you have the outcome that you were thinking the action would have. In our turnover example, you might check the pay relative to others in the organisation with similar skill sets to assess their pay.

Next, you have the ongoing reports. These are helpful, but are simplistic, since they are standard reports. They provide a baseline of information. You can line these ongoing reports together to produce some trends over time. This might be as simple as a headcount report and showing any joiners or leavers from each department.

As we continue to strengthen our measurement power, the next level is benchmarks. How does this one observation compare to others? This provides some context on the issue. A simple example is if your company has 10% turnover and your peer group has 20%. You can assume that you have less volatility in your staff, but do not know the answer to the question 'why is your turnover lower?'

Correlation is the next level and provides greater strength in assessing the issue. In our turnover example, there are many possible factors that can be the cause of turnover: pay relative to market, performance, growth opportunities, management, etc. With correlation measures, you can begin to assess how these factors correlate to turnover and which one might be more highly correlated with departures. However, correlation is not causation.

Up to now, these previous measures are looking at what has happened in the past (i.e. looking through the rear-view mirror). The strongest measures are prediction, causation and simulations. Since these techniques are more valuable, they can be leveraged to make more impactful decisions. These measures look through the windshield, that is, to the future. In our example of turnover, we can ask the question, who is most likely to leave the company? With the answer to this, you can make actions that will address these at-risk employees in a proactive way.

5. **Make a difference**
Business acumen is not reading this book and adding tools to your skills. It is about thinking differently as a business person and not in a traditional HR approach. One of the first things to do is focus on fact-based decision-making. You will get more support for your work if you provide the analytical backup that you will be able to carry out after reading this book. Ultimately, you will be able to make a positive difference to your organisation!

Read the book, enjoy it! You will upgrade your capabilities and immediately start to apply what you learn. As a practitioner, I plan to recommend this book as a baseline reading for HR analytics.

Steve Brink
Chief Executive Officer, Associates for International Research, Inc. (AIRINC)

ACKNOWLEDGMENTS

This book is dedicated to all our students, teaching assistants and colleagues, past and present, who inspire us to push further to make HR practices ever more accessible to the practitioners and their bosses.

We also want to acknowledge the following individuals for all their help in putting this book together: Alexis Saussinan (Merck), Kaj Peltonen and KJ Kim (Tableau), Richard Lee and David Hope (Workday), Eric Sandosham (Red & White Consulting Partners), CheeTung Leong & Dorothy Yiu (EngageRocket), Desmond Tan & Kelly Chua (DDI), Jacob Tan (Aon), and Samir Bedi (EY). Very special thanks to Sid Mehta (Mercer) for all his help in the early conception of the books and early drafts of the material. And to Louisa Lau for her support in the transcriptions of many hours of discussions.

INTRODUCTION

If you torture the data long enough, it will confess!!

— *Ronald Coase, Nobel Prize Winning Economist*

The future of the HR profession lies in analytics. No professional entering the field can expect to succeed in his or her career without a solid understanding and hands-on practice of analytical tools to help in making people decisions.

To implement their business strategies effectively, leaders must deal with people issues in a way that allows them to gain competitive advantage through people (Thomas, Smith, & Diez, 2013). The organisations that will win the 'war for talent' will be those which are better at identifying and keeping key talent, motivating high performance, developing and promoting staff and predicting future people needs accurately. HR professionals need analytics to address these challenges. For example, linking pay for performance has been a dogma of management, but recent research shows that most incentive plans do not produce the desired behaviour, and that pay, in fact, has little correlation to business results (Boudreau, 2010; Diez 2018).

To succeed in the business world, it is imperative that HR provide data-driven answers and insights on how to implement and execute strategy through the people in the organisation. The aim of this book is to arm individual practitioners with practical, hands-on approaches to connect HR policies and practices to business performance. Our objective is to make HR analytics possible for everyone, although some prior knowledge of basic statistics, managerial accounting and HR concepts are useful when reading this book.

We leverage on key statistics and finance concepts, such as ROI and people productivity. We also assume readers are familiar with common available tools (e.g. Workday, Tableau, Excel, etc.) to manage data and visualise outcomes. Throughout the book we discuss data collection, clean-up and warehousing; how to build descriptive and predictive models; and apply HR analytics skills and tools for workforce planning, recruitment, compensation, training, career planning and turnover analysis.

More specifically, by the time readers finish reading this book, they should be able to:

1. Review key statistical and finance/accounting concepts in a way that is useful for HR analytics. These include measures of profit (EBIT, EBITDA, Net Profit), measures of financial return (ROI, ROE, ROA), measures of efficiency (cost, labour productivity) and descriptive/predictive statistics (regressions, correlations, z-scores).

2. Understand basic HR analytics concepts such as data-analytic thinking, data management and modelling. This will allow readers to go beyond the best practices or the benchmark data that HR and its business clients have been relying on to design programs and policies. Using data-analytic thinking and applying it on your own company's data will uncover unique insights that will provide your organisation a competitive edge that the conventional best practices or benchmark data fail to offer.

3. Understand how data are to be collected, prepared for analysis and stored so they can be used with the various commonly found tools.

4. Model HR analytics questions on workforce planning, recruiting, training, career planning, pay and turnover rates.

Our emphasis is in developing the readers' abilities to sell their solutions to the business, and not only understanding of the existing problems through evidence-based management.

How this Book is Organised

In the first four chapters of the book we focus on the basics of HR analytics: Data-analytic thinking, tools, data management and modelling. Once readers have a basic understanding of analytics, we move – in the second part of the book – to the application of these techniques to specific HR problems. Note that we go from simpler analytics to more complex and use a variety of HR issues to illustrate different types of analysis that can be done. Of course, once readers are familiar with various concepts, they can apply them to different HR issues. For instance, we illustrate the use of simple regressions in the chapter about turnover. And we look at multiple regressions when looking at recruiting. But, of course, either concept can be applied to both these HR problems.

Following are the chapter topics and some comments about the broad objectives of each.

Part I: The Basics of HR Analytics

Chapter 1: Basics of Finance and Statistics and Data-analytic Thinking

In this chapter, we review concepts with which you should be familiar, but we cast them in an HR light. These include potential variables of interest such as measures of profit (EBIT, EBITDA, Net Profit), measures of financial return (ROI, ROE, ROA) and measures of efficiency (cost, labour productivity). We also review concepts related to descriptive/predictive statistics (regressions, correlations, z-scores). Finally, we cover the principles of data-analytic thinking, including clustering, text analytics, network science and classification and regression.

Chapter 2: Tools for HR Analytics

The objective of this chapter is to have a look at what popular and easy-to-use tools for HR analytics can do.

Chapter 3: Data Collection, Clean-up and Warehousing

This chapter is about understanding data and how to use them. We discuss structured (internal) data, big data (external), and how to ensure the validity, reliability and generalisability of data for consistency and clarity. We will also talk about storing of data, so it can be consolidated and accessed.

Chapter 4: HR Analytics Modelling
We cover two main ideas in this chapter:

1. Developing and testing hypotheses and models

2. Data analytical thinking

Part II: Applications

Chapter 5: Turnover
Turnover is where most HR analytics programs are focused in practice. We look at a simple, yet powerful, way to address this issue.

Chapter 6: Training and Development
This section considers the important, but elusive, concept of the ROI of training.

Chapter 7: Workforce Planning
Accurately predicting how many employees are needed, with which characteristics and by when, is a source of competitive advantage. We explore how this is done.

Chapter 8: Recruiting
Attracting staff is an essential task of HR. The objective of this chapter is to examine what it takes to 'hire' successful employees, in terms of quality, longevity and fit.

Chapter 9: Pay Plans
Pay is the traditional 'data-driven' area of HR. We explore how HR analytics can be used to ascertain the perceived value of benefit programs.

Chapter 10: Career Planning
In this chapter, we illustrate the importance of setting career tracks and how analytics can be used to support this important HR process.

Chapter 11: HR Policies vs Profit

This chapter brings to light the links between HR policies and company profitability.

Chapter 12: Where to Next?

To conclude, we point readers towards ways to improve their HR analytics skills and additional tools to consider.

PART I: THE BASICS OF HR ANALYTICS

1

BASICS OF FINANCE, STATISTICS AND DATA-ANALYTIC THINKING

1.1 LEARNING OBJECTIVES OF THIS CHAPTER

In this chapter, we will first talk about why the Human Resources (HR) profession needs to embrace analytics, and speak business language, if it is truly to get the much coveted 'seat at the table' which dominates much of the discussion about the importance of HR. The next sections cover the eight-step methodology to be used when addressing HR analytics problems. We will then delve into basic financial and statistical concepts needed to address HR problems in a business context.

We conclude with a case story, explaining how and why this large multinational has implemented HR analytics as part of its people strategies.

1.2 THE CHANGING NATURE OF HR

As organisations seek to improve performance, the onus is on HR to build value. The well-worn phrases about 'People are our greatest assets' and about 'HR being the ultimate competitive advantage', can be true when the HR function focuses on solving business problems as opposed to people problems.

The HR profession is still struggling with this idea of having a seat at the senior management table. The answer to this question is, yes, it can, if HR can speak the same language as the rest of the senior management team. As long as HR professionals continue to talk about people turnover and employee engagement as the key metrics in HR, other senior executives will continue to think that, for HR, it is people's emotions that drive business. Senior executives speak in numbers, financial and otherwise. If HR wants to be heard, it needs to be able to put HR arguments in business language, meaning, using data that link HR decisions to business outcomes. This is the key. Otherwise, discussions between HR and the line becomes one person's 'gut' versus somebody else's 'gut'. HR runs the risk of being ignored if it cannot present a credible business case. This is where HR analytics helps HR to become a credible business partner: showing up with a set of well-thought-out numbers will go a long way.

Today's HR Function is expected to provide senior leadership with more information to run the business, and also provide more personalised services to employees. These demands encapsulate the arguments for the need of HR analytics in organisations: On the one hand, the HR professional that has a handle on analytics is better positioned to answer business questions from top management (e.g. 'Which profile of our sales force will best help us to increase sales revenue?'). On the other hand, HR analytics tools can also help deliver a better employment experience to employees (e.g. 'Which combination of employee benefits and work–life balance programmes delivers highest staff engagement?'). As data are more readily available than ever, HR is being asked **for more information, better insights**, and **more precise recommendations** to help run their businesses. It is by understanding the underlying business issues and delivering on these requests, that the HR Function can best claim the 'seat at the table' it rightly deserves. Fig. 1.1 below illustrates the changing HR requests from management.

1.3 WHY HR ANALYTICS NOW?

In 2016, Deloitte's report on Global Human Capital Trends (https://www2.deloitte.com/content/dam/Deloitte/global/Documents/HumanCapital/gx-dup-global-human-capital-trends-2016.pdf)

	Traditional	Current	Future
Recruitment	"I need to fill a position. What is the process?"	"I need to fill a position. Where can we find the best talent for this role? And, how do we identify if the talent is culturally fit for our organisation as well as our team?"	"I am hoping to strengthen my talent pipeline. Can you recommend some suitable candidates who are the best fit to our organisation as well as our team?"
Rewards	"What is the employee benefits in the organisation?"	"Can we find out what our employees want and tailor our benefits to different age group, marital status, and location?"	"Can we push notifications to our employees about the benefits that meet both their lifestyle needs as well as our needs in the organisation?"
Attrition	"Someone from my team has resigned. Can we revise his salary package to match the competitor's offer?"	"Someone from my team has resigned. Since exit interview revealed that salary is the top reason of attrition, let's give him an increment."	"What are the key attrition drivers for top performers from various age group?"
Learning and Development	"What courses are available for my team members?"	"Could you add an online course into the learning system to help my team member with a sales meeting next month?"	"Can you notify my team members of their learning needs over the next 18 months? Please recommend development actions similar profile have taken in the past."
Succession Planning	"How many successors are there for this leadership role?"	"Who are the best leaders with the right values in our organization?"	"What traits, skills and competencies do we need in order to drive our organization's strategic priorities?"

Fig. 1.1. Changing HR Requests from Management.

revealed that 77% of all organisations believe people analytics (PA) is important, and 32% of the participating companies felt ready or somewhat ready for analytics – a slight increase from 24% the previous year.

According to Deloitte's Global Human Capital Trends 2017 (https://www2.deloitte.com/content/dam/Deloitte/global/Documents/About-Deloitte/central-europe/ce-global-human-capital-trends.pdf), a majority of companies (71%) who participated in the study continued to report that PA is a high priority in their organisation. However, only 9% agreed that they have good understanding of which talent dimensions drive performance in their organisations; and only 15% reported to have widely deployed talent scorecards for their line managers, evidencing a slow adoption of analytics.

Despite the collection of a wide range of data from various sources, many organisations today are not effectively leveraging their data for HR analytics. Why? Deloitte's study revealed that more than 80% of HR professionals score themselves low in their ability to analyse. This is a troubling fact in an increasingly data-driven field.

For new HR professionals, analytics will become the price of entry into the profession. For existing HR professionals, analytics is the minimum expected to be able to have strategic conversations about the impact HR has in the implementation of the business' strategy.

1.4 TYPES OF ANALYSIS

There are three main types of analysis that can be done with data.

1. **Descriptive Analysis.** Answers the question: 'What happened?' This type of analysis summarises raw data to understand what has occurred, based on historical data, and helps to uncover patterns that can offer insights to explain the reasons for the occurrence. This allows to learn from past behaviours and understand how they might influence future outcomes.

2. **Diagnostics.** Answers the question: 'Why did it happen?' In this type of analysis typically there are measures about the relationship between two variables, and the motivation is to go beyond 'what happened' to understanding 'what was the driver or explanation for what happened?'. This knowledge can then allow us to take actions that reinforce a desired outcome or mitigate against an undesired one. For instance, job satisfaction vs retention; engagement vs profitability; culture vs turnover; ethics vs profit; job satisfaction vs customer satisfaction; etc.

3. **Predictive Analysis.** Answers the question: 'What is likely to happen?' Uses a variety of statistical techniques to determine the probable future outcome of an event, or the likelihood of a situation occurring. Note that, different than in the above-mentioned diagnostic analysis, there is a clear implication on the direction of causation. A causal relationship exists where the occurrence of one event is linked to another. For example, recruiting source predicts retention; changes in LinkedIn profile predicts absenteeism; training programmes predicts sales outcomes; projected return on investment (ROI) of a new talent retention solution; forecast ROI of new compensation arrangements.

Fig. 1.2 illustrates the continuum of HR Analytics Maturity, from the least to the most powerful. The descriptive techniques are often based on anecdotes ('Our managers say that the lack of compensation competitiveness is causing attrition on their team'), reactive

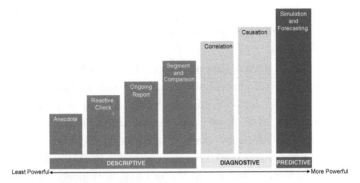

Fig. 1.2. HR Analytics Maturity.

checks ('Exit interviews confirm that pay is the reason our employees are leaving'), ongoing reports ('Our engagement scores are lower than last year'), or segment and comparison, which can be from internal data or from external benchmarking.

('Our competitor is providing 80 hours of training per employee vs our current rate of 40 per employee'). In all these cases, there is an explanation of what has happened, but insufficient information about how to address it. Even in the last example where there are data apparently supporting more training, there is no information as to whether this is helping the competitor, or if it would help the company.

Diagnostics are more powerful than the ongoing reports because they are motivated to understand the primary drivers of an outcome of interest, such that when actions are taken on the important drivers the likelihood of improving outcomes is materially positive. Employee engagement studies are often a good example of diagnostic analytics. These would point us to top drivers of engagement to nudge us into prioritising our follow-up actions. The initial construct assumes that employee engagement can be influenced by several factors: top leadership effectiveness, direct manager effectiveness, career advancement opportunities, learning and development opportunities, competitive pay and benefits, relationships at work, etc. The diagnostic analytics helps to determine which are the factors that indeed have the biggest relative influence on engagement. This in turn allows HR and the leadership team to help prioritise on the few factors that, when acted upon, will have a material impact on improving engagement.

It is easy to assume that one causes the other, but it could be that another factor affects both, and just looking at these two sets of data does not consider this possibility. Thus, we say the data are correlated, even if we often ascribe directionality to these kinds of results. A clearer example of causality is the impact that providing training to line employees on quality issues can have on manufacturing cost reduction. We can say, definitively, that the training helped to reduce costs, even if it may not be exact figures.

Predictive analytics will help forecast what would happen if we do this or don't do that. How much we expect sales volume to change if we change the commission structure of the sales force? This is the type of data the business leaders are most eager to receive, but also the hardest to produce.

The three types of analysis are useful, however, so it's important to know and use them all, but with some caution! Some enthusiastic HR teams and professionals may fall into the trap of jumping straight into their data and profess about their analytics prowess, without identifying the right problems that these powerful tools should be wielded upon.

The power of analytics resides not in the sophisticated tools but on the thoughtful identification of problems to which these tools are applied.

A 'rookie' mistake often made by those new to analytics is to spend most of their time and energy on mining data with new, sophisticated tools. The lure of 'fancy' and 'cutting-edge' analysis can bedazzle the wisest. But if this search for answers in the data is not solving a problem that has the potential of a lift in business performance or if the insights are not well understood and believed by those that eventually need to act upon the insights derived, then the analysis by itself will have no use for the organisation.

We are therefore keen to equip readers with both the analytical tools and with the mindset, intuition and process to select problems worth solving. These are the foundations to build the capability to turn insights into the behavioural changes necessary to realise the value of HR analytics.

1.5 HR ANALYSTS AS ARCHITECTS

The data analytics process is akin to a house-building analogy as we will describe later. As much as it can be broken down into distinct steps, in reality it is more iterative than linear. To be successful in harnessing the value of data, readers need to embrace – and practice – some crucial mental models in addition to technical skills, which is what makes data science an 'art'.

In the following section we explain what we mean about mental states for successful data science:

Act like an architect more than just an analyst: Once a high-impact problem has been successfully identified, it's important to frame the 'design of analyses' before actually jumping into any analyses. A common mistake HR analytics teams make is to jump into data gathering and analyses without thinking about what needs to be analysed to solve their problem.

Just as an architect starts with a blueprint, and not the bricks, when building a house, you need a clear blueprint for your analyses before the data and the analyses. This blueprint is the 'design of analyses'. This 'thinking process' is to be carried out before any data collection or analyses.

When hiring an architect to build a house, the expectation is that the architect will produce a blueprint of the house, which reflects the client's functional and emotional needs. The owner and the architect don't start the building process until the detailed blueprint has been signed off; this ensures that resources (time and money) are not wasted downstream.

The architect and the client go through several iterations, which involve revised versions about not just functional needs and constraints but also how the client reacts to the models of the end product that the architect mocks up as he interprets these needs. The iterative nature of this process is fundamental in building the financial and emotional security that the project sponsor needs to commit to a massive undertaking.

As the owner of the analytics project, you also need to act like the architect who engages the client in the design process before building the house. As an architect, the aim should be to achieve two goals, right up front in the analytics project:

1. Gain clarity for an envisioned end-state of the project.

2. Secure the buy-in of your project sponsor.

Focus on changing behaviour rather than just generating insights: Data analytics projects often start with the notion that the goal is to generate insights. Successful projects recognise the limitation of that notion. It is better to focus on the behavioural changes the project aims to affect, rather than just the insights it can produce. HR analysts are happy to move from project to project because they love 'doing the analyses', but project sponsors care more about the 'results'. Results emerge only when insights are acted upon.

Generating a conversation about the behavioural change HR analytics projects seek to achieve will provide clarity about the following:

- Who will be the end user (/s) of the end product?

- Will the outcome enable a decision, or would it be an input into another workflow for the end user?

- How best to present the end product?

- What training will be needed to provide for effective application of the end product?

- How often should the outcome be updated for it to remain relevant?

Well-thought-out answers to the abovementioned questions will allow the project team and the project sponsor to gain a deeper and a more action-oriented appreciation for the project outcomes and what needs to happen to eventually improve business performance (Guenole, Ferrar, & Feinzig, 2017). This is the 'use phase' of the project and this is what happens when insights get acted upon by the end user of the HR analytics project. Thinking about the 'use phase' enables a more practical vision for the end product. Another positive by-product of this discussion is the discovery of other units the project outcomes depend on. While the analytics team is focused on generating insights, the IT team can be called in to create the right user interface (UI) for an application where insights can be embedded into, for the end users to make decisions. Line leaders may also be called upon to train their staff about the new workflow that incorporates the HR analytics data-based insights. The IT team could also create a reporting tool to capture the frequency of decisions that align with the recommendation and the consequent end results they affected. If the recommendations indeed produce the intended results, but only a small fraction of the staff acted in line with the recommendations, there is more work left in effecting the adoption of a new data-based decision-making tool. On the other hand, if the tracking suggests that the recommendations don't affect the intended results, then the team has not quite generated the right insights and there is more work to be done in the data analyses phase before the end user can adopt the recommendations.

Clarity about the use phase of a project is an important step in creating action-oriented outcomes rather than scientifically sound, theoretically rich insights that no one acts upon.

Be a great social architect: In addition to being deliberate about the intellectual quality of the 'design of analyses', it is important to think about the social architecture to be used to effect adoption of the end product.

The extent to which sponsors (both business owners that are experiencing the problem being solved and those providing the budgets to carry out the project) and potential end users have been involved in the 'design' and 'validation' of project blueprint and interim deliverables will determine the success in not just creating an intelligent solution but also one which is actively embraced and adopted.

Answers to the following questions will help to design a social architecture for success:

- Who are the important stakeholders for this project? (sponsors, users, technical gatekeepers, coaches.)

- What may be their motivation regarding the project and how can it be used to gain their support?

- What may be the order of priority, regarding the multiple goals the project needs to fulfil?

- How to gain consensus regarding the few things that matter most?

- When to be 'prescriptive' rather than 'facilitative'?

- Who should be engaged and what may be the most efficient process to improve the quality of insight and the social ownership for downstream success?

Iterate quickly and learn through feedback loops: As much as we have emphasised the need to 'think' more than 'doing' upfront in the process, it is important to realise that that mindset should not become too rigid. Successful projects allow for quick prototyping and feedback from end users. In the analyses phase of most projects, constraints will pop up (lack of data or poor quality of data) that will require going back to change the design and sometimes even redefine the problem statement and the envisioned end product.

For professionals not accustomed to this iterative process, the need to go back to the sponsors and end users again can become a source of embarrassment and be seen as a failure. However, in the analytics process, there are many unknowns and the desire to be 'perfect' and 'right the first time' for each step of the process may actually be an obstacle.

Instead, it's best to find a way to move through the entire eight-step process described below, as 'iterative loops' rather than 'sequential steps'. The ability to move through these loops quickly is a key ingredient to success.

1.6 AN EIGHT-STEP APPROACH TO HR ANALYTICS

The following eight-step process will help to tackle any type of analytics problem (see Fig. 1.3 overleaf):

1.6.1 Define the Business Problem

This step is critical to ensure that the analytics project is necessary and able to solve the burning issues in the organisation. It also serves to avoid analytics team focusing on the wrong analysis.

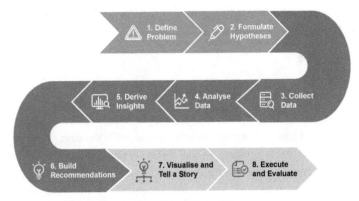

Fig. 1.3. An Eight-step Approach to HR Analytics.

First, it's important to have an understanding of the business as the basis of framing questions. With a strong understanding of how the business works, you will be able to understand the context and ask the right questions when the line raises a request for something.

Second, reach out to the right stakeholders and use consulting techniques, such as questioning, listening and paraphrasing, to get to the heart of the problem. Through conversations, seek for clarity and ensure the business problem is properly understood and defined in their terms and yours.

One last thing in this step is to be sure to obtain agreement on the business issue the analytics project will address. It is wise to document the business issue and seek endorsement from the project sponsor. For instance, in addition to the potential to lift performance, as HR analytics teams start their journey, they should also consider the likelihood of solving the problem with the current time frame, data and tools available. If the team chooses a very difficult problem, even if it has a huge potential to lift performance, chances are that, in time, the team will lose the mindshare of the leadership team if it failed. Thus, to be able to judge if the problem is solvable within a reasonable time and budget is as important a skill upfront as any. It is better to go for solvable problems with relatively lower impact than a low-probability ('unsolvable') problem offering a high return. The team should focus on building a positive momentum of successes to gain the sponsorship and mindshare of executives. With earned credibility, it is possible to go after more difficult problems downstream.

1.6.2 Formulate Hypotheses

Formulating hypotheses is vital for testing beliefs about the causes of business issues. A strong hypothesis will guide the data gathering and data analysis process, as well as protecting the analytics team from reaching a false conclusion based on observed relationships in the data.

Here are some useful tips to follow when formulating hypotheses:

- State a clear claim that you want to test. Hypotheses are pro-vocative and reflect your belief; these cannot be placid neutral statements. A good hypothesis describes a clear relationship between an outcome of interest and its underlying cause. An example of a poor hypothesis is as follows:

    Our pay for performance differentiation is not right.

- While the above hypothesis states a claim, it is suggesting that something is ineffective about 'pay differentiation', it does not clarify the 'so what?'. If we don't know the effect of the claim, we cannot test the hypothesis. A better statement would be the following:

    The lack of pay differentiation leads to attrition of our staff.

- User experience and relevant literature can accelerate the hypothesis development process. The analytics team may use existing information (such as pulse survey responses, exit interviews, employee engagement results) in the organisation as a basis for hypotheses formulation. Alternatively, the team could reference the latest scientific thinking in academic journals to understand the causes for the phenomenon that are being studied. In addition, engagement with the organ-isational stakeholders and end users through interviews or focus group discussions could provide insights about potential causes for the problem and accelerate the hypotheses formulation.

- Make sure the hypotheses are testable. Ultimately, the analytics team needs to prove, or disprove, the hypotheses. For instance, when making a claim that training customer service agents on 'listening skills' improves the customer experience, the team will need data on both 'customer experience' and 'listening skills' training to test this relationship.

- The number of times a hypothesis should be tested depends on the rigour of the analysis design, the availability and quality of data, the budget assigned to the analysis and the time available, among other variables. Keep in mind that numerous results supporting the hypothesis can be overturned by one single additional test that disproves it.

- Avoid over-complication. In order to answer some business issues, it is likely that more than one hypothesis will be involved. However, multiple hypotheses could complicate the analysis. Therefore, it is best to rationalise the number of hypotheses where possible, to reduce complexity.

1.6.3 Collect Data

This step is to identify the most relevant data for testing the hypotheses and determining if data quality is sufficient to proceed. This process will also inform the business on new data that need to be collected moving forward.

Here are some tips for data collection:

- Be objective-driven. When performing data cleaning, new areas of exploration could emerge. Don't get lost in data; always stay on track and be reminded of the business issues that the analytic team is determined to answer.

- Map out data needs prior to data gathering. Begin with mapping out data and undertake some checks before gathering it, to ensure that it contains unique identifiers to link the data sets that the team plans to analyse.

- Focus on data that are available. Start with data that are already available in the organisation (or open sourced). Evaluate the data quality for hypothesis testing before collecting more (or new) data.

- Think carefully about new data. If a new data set is required, think carefully about how to collect it. Remember: a small amount of new, high-quality data is better than a large amount of semi-useful data.

Fig. 1.4 illustrates this process.

1.6.4 Analyse Data

This is where the methodology and statistics are applied to data to test the hypotheses and provide the basis for insights.

Various analytical methods and associated technologies (please see sections below as well as the next chapter on tools) can make analysis more focused and successful.

Selecting the right technology and most appropriate method for analysis requires a basic knowledge of what the various methods and technologies can deliver.

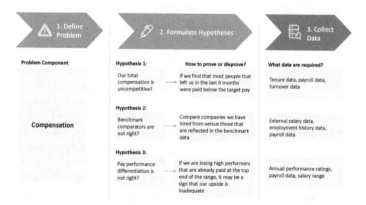

Fig. 1.4. Example of an Analysis Design Framework.

1.6.5 Derive Insights

This step requires the analytics team to derive and show the most pertinent insights from the data and analysis. Presenting only data and analysis results to business line executives may result in flawed conclusions that fit individuals' preconceptions. Data are useful, and analytical results are interesting; but understanding the context of the results is what leads to insights.

Here are some tips:

- Summarise insights in one sentence
- Present insights using visuals (more on that in Chapter 2)
- Avoid displaying raw data or analysis
- Articulate why insights are important

1.6.6 Build Recommendations

A great insight will lose its meaning if recommendations to improve the business are not made. Many projects fail at this stage because recommendations are not expressed clearly.

Below are some tips for making recommendations:

- One recommendation for each insight. This allows the analytics team to clarify why the insight is important and how the business is impacted if something is done about it.
- Make a clear statement for each recommendation. Each one should be simple, clear and straightforward.
- Group recommendations into main themes. Upon deriving all recommendations from insights, group the recommendations into related topics to make it easier to see how they will work together to solve the business problem.

1.6.7 Visualise and Tell a Story

Storytelling is the connection between the analyses, the data and the executives. Analytics truly adds value when the team can explain this connection.

Once your recommendations are grouped into themes, you can craft a story that explains how these recommendations will play out. Graphs and visualisation tools can be very helpful in telling a cohesive story.

Avoid the 'In the beginning...' syndrome. You have seen this before: The analytics team starts where they started, and want to walk the audience through every step of the process, pausing for emphasis in all the places where they had difficulty and showing via sheer volume the amount of work and cleverness that they had to put into it. Not too many slides into it, the audience is checking their phones for emails, or anything else, to pass the time until you get to the conclusions. Then they look up again.

To avoid this trap, one useful recommendation is to start your presentation at the end and then explain the main reasons why you think it makes sense: 'We think the answer to this problem is to do Recommendations X, Y and Z. Let me first explain why Recommendation X: It is (show the appropriate graph) of Insight X. Let me now explain why Recommendation Y...' And so on. Leave out anything else that is not critical. At this point you are not trying to show how much work you did, but trying to sell a solution.

Here are some additional tips:

- Synthesise the data. To be sure, distilling the analysis down to the key items is often harder than the analysis itself. And there is no way around it: Pick the most important elements and leave the rest out! You can always put the full data into the appendix, in case there is a question!

- Provide context. Connect the facts and insights of your data and analysis to provide that context.

- Create structure. Stories without structure appear disorganised. Often the issue is that the linkages are not clear because there are too many data and not all of it is connected. With structure, data and insights support each other in a way that makes the story simple to understand and act upon.

- Sell it! It's a sales job at this point; no longer an analytical project. Analytics got you this far, but your ability to tell the story is the clincher.

As an example, a company was looking to determine which profile of sales force made most sense in its growth strategy. HR interviewed several sales managers and discovered that each of them had their own preferred profile for a sales person, and there was no consensus, nor any evidence that any of these approaches worked better than any other. The HR team collected data on sales results for each of the sales people in the last three years and combined it with information from the HRIS as well as other internal systems. After months of analysis they had a great deal of insights and numbers to show, but restricted their presentation on the results to a handful of slides which basically started with 'Do you want to increase sales results by X% over the next 12–18 months? If you do, you need to change the profile of your sales force so that it matches these attributes A, B, C and D.' They were prepared to answer any question that came up, as they expected pushback from the veteran sales managers who had 'always done it this way'. To their surprise, there were no questions whatsoever! After a long silence, the CEO said 'Ok, it's agreed, let's do this!', and moved on to the next topic on the agenda. A big day for the HR team! After 12–18 months, the team went to evaluate the results and discovered that, in those regions that had changed the sales force to the indicated profile, sales results had actually exceeded the estimate.

1.6.8 Execute and Evaluate

There are a few items to consider prior to the implementation of the recommendations:

- Seek for endorsement. Communicate with stakeholders to gain agreement on clear decisions; identify owners of action plan and ensure stakeholder commitment

- Embed change management. Depending on the scope of recommendations, change management needs to be included as part of the action plan to ensure results are fully delivered

- Team up with the HR business partners (HRBPs). Work closely with HRBPs to determine the impact of implementation on people

- Set milestones. Consider the timing of evaluation: short- and long-term impacts of project; set milestone for reflection and determine the success of the entire project

- Secure a project sponsor. A project sponsor is someone who has an active interest in one or more analytics projects, responsible for approving the project, coordinating resources for project execution, advocating for the project and communicating with stakeholders to ensure that actions are properly implemented. A strong project sponsor is usually a highly respected leaders in the organisation, with deep understanding of the organisation and the challenges it is facing, is well connected and able to rally support for the project, is willing and able to secure the resources required and is highly motivated and available to see the project through to its completion and benefits realisation. The sponsor is more involved in defining the business problem, formulating the hypotheses, telling stories with insights and the evaluation steps. And less so in the analysis of data.

It is crucial to monitor the implementation results over time (short-, mid- and long term), to determine if things worked out as planned, and identify the need to refresh the analysis or research, ensuring the analytics project delivers exactly in the way it is intended.

By adding this step after the 'conclusion' of each analytics project, the HR team can ensure that:

- The right decisions are made and implemented as a result of the analytics project

- The action plan is based on these decisions

- The project has generated value to the organisation

1.7 WHY DO SOME ANALYTICS PROJECTS FAIL?

According to Forbes (https://www.forbes.com/sites/piyanka jain/2015/12/12/5-reasons-why-analytics-projects-fail/#41d00c0 c6507), the top five reasons why analytics projects fail are as follows:

- Starting with data, not questions: Not having prior hypotheses is a dangerous proposition for an analytics project. Given the abundance of data you'd be able to access, you can easily get distracted into doing interesting analyses which add little value to the problem you are trying to solve. Upfront hypotheses generation can not only keep you focused but also make you efficient as a team. The most common misunderstanding about analytics is that, if you look at data hard enough, you will find insights.

- Unengaged stakeholders/sponsors: Working with the wrong or absent stakeholders (i.e. the decision-makers and owners of the business processes) leads to weak hypotheses, long cycles of analysis and limited/low credibility insights.

- Using an exploratory approach to analytics: An exploratory approach often fails to find insights and if it does, it is a lengthy process. On the other hand, using hypotheses to narrow down the project scope and the data set required leads to the answers faster.

- Weak hypotheses: Failure to follow due process with the right stakeholders will often lead to wrong assumptions and inadequate or incomplete hypotheses.

- Inaccessible or bad data: The data do not need to be perfect for a successful analytics project, just cleaner and with fewer data issues. Data maturity is thus a prerequisite for analytics maturity.

1.8 FINANCE FOR HR PROFESSIONALS

HR professionals may not need to know all the details of finance, but to be taken seriously at a strategic level, confidence with financial jargon is essential. At a minimum, HR is required to understand how revenue is made, how profit is affected by cash flows, be explicit about the labour components of revenue and costs and be able to ask informed questions when necessary.

The following section is a summary of key terms of finance that all HR professionals should know. Of course, this is not a finance book; please consult the appropriate literature if you would like to delve deeper into these concepts.

1.8.1 Profit Measures

- Revenue: Volume × Price

- Gross Profit: Revenue − Cost of Goods Sold

- EBIT: Earnings Before Interest and Taxes; Gross Profit − Expenses

- EBITDA: Earnings Before Interest, Taxes, Depreciation and Amortization; EBIT + Depreciation + Amortization

- Net Income/Profit: EBIT − Interest − Taxes

1.8.2 Market and Other Common Performance Measures

- Earnings Per Share (EPS): Company's profit divided by the number of common outstanding shares. Used to compare performance with prior years and with other potential investments

- Return on Net Assets (RONA): Company profits divided by the net assets. Measures the use of assets

- Return on Equity (ROE): The amount of net income returned as a percentage of shareholder equity; measures company's profitability by revealing how much profit they generate with the money shareholders have invested

- Total Shareholder Return (TSR): Share price appreciation and dividends paid in a specific period. Measures the performance of different companies' stocks and shares over time. Can be absolute or relative.

- Economic Value Added (EVA): Measure of a company's financial performance based on the residual wealth calculated by deducting its cost of capital from its operating profit, adjusted for taxes on a cash basis.

- Weighted Average Cost of Capital (WACC): The cost of money to a company. Calculated by weighing the cost of borrowed money and the cost of shareholder equity (the latter estimated as opportunity cost – what shareholders could receive if they invested in another venture with a similar risk profile).

1.8.3 Cost-related Terms

- Fixed Costs: Do not vary for each dollar of revenue. For example, corporate staff (salaried, consistently hourly schedules), audit fees, basic repair and maintenance costs, rent.

- Variable Costs: Vary for each dollar of revenue, often at a relatively consistent rate. For example, hourly staff (variable schedules), sales compensation, costs of running machines, raw materials costs, shipping expenses.

1.9 RECAP ON STATISTICS CONCEPTS

1.9.1 Categorical and Continuous Variables

- Nominal: Data with two or more categories, but which do not have an intrinsic order

- Dichotomous: Data with only two categories or levels

- Ordinal: Data that have a fixed, small (<100) number of possible values, called levels, that are ordered or ranked

- Interval: Data have a central characteristic and can be measured along a continuum with a numerical value

- Ratio: Interval variables, but with the added condition that 0 (zero) of the measurement indicates that there is none of that variable

1.9.2 Measures of Central Location

- Mean: Excel function: =AVERAGE(data range); Outliers can affect the value of the mean

- Median: Excel function =MEDIAN(data range); Specifies the middle value when the data are arranged from least to greatest. The median is meaningful for ratio, interval and ordinal data. Will not be affected by outliers

- Mode: Excel function: =MODE.SNGL(data range); The observation that occurs most frequently. Most useful for data sets that contain a relatively small number of unique values. In a frequency distribution, it is the value or group having the largest frequency. In a histogram, it is the highest bar.

- Midrange: Excel function: =MIN and MAX functions. The average of the greatest and least values in the data set. Extreme values easily distort the result because the midrange uses only two pieces of data, whereas the mean uses all the data; thus, it is usually a much rougher estimate than the mean and is often used for only small sample sizes.

1.9.3 Measures of Dispersion

- Range: Excel Formula: = MAX − MIN. The difference between the maximum value and the minimum value in the data set

- Interquartile Range: It is the difference between the first and third quartiles; this measure includes only the middle 50% of the data and, therefore, is not influenced by extreme values.

- Variance: The 'average' of the squared deviations from the mean. Excel function for population = VAR.P(data range); For sample = VAR.Sdata range). Note that in Excel, the formula for population divides by N, whereas the formula for sample divides by $N - 1$.

- Standard Deviation: The square root of the variance. In Excel, for population = STDEV.P(data range);

For sample = STDEV.S(data range). A higher standard deviation means more variability in the data.

- Z-score: It provides a relative measure of the distance an observation is from the mean, which is independent of the units of measurement. Excel function: =STANDARDIZE(x, mean, standard_dev). Example:

  - a z-score of 1.0 means that the observation is one standard deviation to the right of the mean;

  - a z-score of −1.5 means that the observation is 1.5 standard deviations to the left of the mean.

1.9.4 Measures of Association

- Correlation: is a measure of the linear relationship between two variables, X and Y, which does not depend on the units of measurement. It is measured by the correlation coefficient, which is scaled between −1 and 1. Excel function: =CORREL(array1,array2).

- R2 (R-squared): is a measure of the 'fit' of the line to the data. The value of R2 will be between 0 and 1. A value of 1.0 indicates a perfect fit and all data points would lie on the line; the larger the value of R2, the better the fit.

- Standard Error: is the variability between observed and predicted Y values.

1.9.5 Population and Sampling

- A population is defined as all the items in the set of data to be analysed. For instance, all employees in the company when looking at overall trends, or all employees in manufacturing, if you are looking specifically at the manufacturing employees

- Note that, if you are looking at how manufacturing employees compare to all other employees, then the population is 'all employees' and, therefore, 'manufacturing employees' is a subset of this population

- A sample is thus defined as a subset of a population. In statistics we often work with samples, as it is faster and less costly than to deal with whole populations. For example, in collecting salary data, the population would be defined as all incumbents in all companies for the job you are analysing. In practice, we use salary surveys that only have a fraction of the whole market in their database. Another example is in engagement surveys, where the population would be all employees in the company but, in practice, we look only at a percentage of this population.

- The process of using sample data to estimate population data in a way that is representative of the whole population relies heavily on the quality of the sample. With random sampling, data items from the population are selected into the sample by chance, thus improving the probability of the sample being representative of the population. However, we often have to rely on non-random sampling for convenience. In which case, we must be mindful of possible sampling errors and confidence intervals.

1.9.6 Statistical Forecasting Models

- A **regression analysis** allows for the development of statistical models that show the strength of the relationship between the dependent variable and one or more independent variables. Generally, regressions are categorised as:

  - Simple regressions, which have only one independent variable

  - Multiple regressions, which have two or more independent variables

- Regression as Analysis of Variance (**ANOVA**): conducts a test to determine whether variations in Y are due to varying the levels of X. ANOVAs are typically used to test for significance of regression. Note: Excel reports the p-value (Significance F)

- H0: population slope coefficient = 0 (not a significant variable)

- H1: population slope coefficient ≠ 0 (is a significant variable)

- Rejecting H0 indicates that X explains variation in Y

- **Overfitting:** Fitting a model too closely to the sample data at the risk of not fitting it well to the population in which we are interested. When too many terms are added to the model, the model may not adequately predict other values from the population. Can be mitigated by using good logic, intuition and theory, and parsimony.

- **Time Series:** These are a collection of historical data; for instance, daily production yields. Generally have components such as random behaviour, trends (upward or downward), seasonal effects, cyclical effects.

  - Time series are considered stationary when they only exhibit random behaviour

  - Trends are gradual positive or negative movements of time series.

SUMMARY

In this chapter, we covered the following:

- The evolution of HR analytics

- Analytics maturity model

- The eight-step methodology to approach an analytical project

- Key financial terms and concepts that HR professionals should know

- Basic statistics and various methods for data analysis

We started with the concept that HR analytics helps to answer questions from business leaders about the way in which HR can help grow company revenue and profitability. To successfully apply HR analytics in answering these questions, it is important to have some degree of understanding of statistics and finance, and how to collect, store and use data.

Another skill required is how to build hypotheses. This comes from getting inside the data and determining what kind of story you can build with the result of your analysis. Data-analytic thinking is about that very simple concept of creating hypotheses, testing them and keep validating these hypotheses until you arrive at some good ideas and insights that can be combined into a powerful story. That is exactly what management wants to hear. That's the language the business leaders speak.

QUESTIONS

HR problems are typically clustered around a few main themes or clusters. Below we list a few themes and some questions associated with them. Can you think of additional questions you may want to ask in each cluster?

Workforce Planning

- What is our revenue/profit and annual productivity improvement per employee?
- What skills/competencies does the organisation need now and in the future?
- What is the demographic distribution of the organisation's high performers?
- Are all key roles filled with outstanding performers?
- Are we staffed at the right levels?
- What is the optimum balance among 'build, buy and borrow' strategies for different roles?

Talent Acquisition

- What is the perception of our employment brand among potential candidates?
- Is our employee value proposition compelling for different types of employees, so that they become promoters of our employment brand?
- What percentage of candidates accept our offers?
- Which recruiting channels provide the best employees?
- Are our candidate assessments adequately predicting future success?
- What percentage of new hires remain in the company 36 months later?

Talent Engagement

- What are engagement levels of top talent and employees in key/hard-to-fill jobs?
- Are engagement levels correlated with business outcomes and turnover rates?

Talent Development

- Are training programmes helping to improve individual on-the-job performance?
- What is the ROI of training programmes?
- Which managers have an excellent reputation for being 'talent developers?'

Talent Deployment

- What percentage of employees apply for internal jobs?
- Which departments attract/share internal employees?

Leading and Managing Talent

- What percentage of leaders are promoted internally?

- What is the relative performance of developed vs acquired leaders?

- Which leadership programmes have been more successful in producing excellent leaders?

- Which leaders are better at developing other leaders?

Talent Retention

- What is the 'sweet spot' turnover in various departments of the organisation?

- What is the turnover rate within the first year on the job?

- Is there a pattern of turnover related to tenure with the organisation?

- What is the turnover rate by gender, age, level, tenure, location, department and manager?

- What are the principal reasons for turnover in the organisation?

Setting Up an HR Analytics Team[1]

This German multinational science and technology company has recently set up their PA team. It is led by a French-born executive, who resides in Singapore.

The PA team has helped to raise awareness of the importance of HR analytics by convincing global leaders at the

[1]With thanks to Alexis Saussinan, Head of People Analytics, Consultancy and Organisational Development at Merck Group.

company about how HR analytics can help them to do more informed business and people decisions and by looking into the strategic forward-thinking topics the company is focusing on in the next 5, 10 and 20 years.

A good portion of the PA team's work is to raise awareness to make the business leaders think of their people and HR differently. Part of this process is to make business leaders understand that there are some hypotheses about their employees and their productivity they might be thinking about, but that most of the time they are making decisions based on either gut feel or because they saw or heard something which 'sounded' convincing enough. Since the company wants to move away from this mode of decision-making about people, and towards evidence-based/fact-based/data-based thinking to help drive better and faster business decisions, having a PA team makes sense.

The PA team consists of more than seven people, based in Asia/Pac, Europe and Americas to be close to the business. It operates as a virtual team with the cultural know-how across the regions where the company operates.

The PA team operates under the philosophy that it is critical to understand the businesses in order to speak with HR and business leaders about what the businesses are facing from the HR analytics standpoint. The PA team believes that simply crunching enormous databases to find amazing insights to show the business will not be enough to get them to hear these insights if the businesses are not ready to hear them or if they are not in line with the way they are doing business.

The skill sets within the team are also quite diverse: There are team members who are strong data scientists, other looking at technology and others with data analytics background and consulting experience. The main criterion for selection into the PA team is the ability to listen to the business, translate what they heard into what it could mean from a people standpoint and then making the data 'talk' in a relevant way.

Organisationally, the PA team understands they live in a corporate environment and the importance of staying connected to trends that are happening within and around the company. To leverage all the capabilities available, they are very much integrated with the internal and external ecosystems. That way they can leverage, not only the HR people data at hand, but also how the people data or organisational data are meaningful in the business context, working with business analytics teams (Evans, 2017).

To do analytics well, it takes a bit of time and pre-requisites, especially on the data side. In this case, the journey from the start to a fully functioning PA team took five years. First, they had to consolidate technology and data sources together, which took about two to three years. Like many global organisations, they had a large amount of data sets, usually with different definitions, and stored in various formats. The initial foundational work to start to do HR analytics should not be under-estimated as the time put in at the beginning saves much time later.

Many organisations struggle with their data systems foundation. For example, in a typical organisation where the foundational work has not been done, when a business leader comes with an issue, it can take several months from the time HR first speaks with the business person to the time the initial insights are ready to be shared. This is because they must develop several hypotheses after the first conversation, then identify the data they will need and then collect the data to do the analysis.

In our case, thanks to that foundational work, between the first conversation with a business leader until they come with meaningful information, only takes a few days. In fact, often they can respond in a matter of hours, even minutes. The PA team's technology integrates most employee's data in real time. This is what the foundation work allows them to do: They have employee's life cycle employment data, from pre-hire to exit interview. This means they can check the average time to hire, or the average compensation per employee from the whole company down to the very latest hire anywhere in the world, if they want to. The live data are refreshed every month.

However, the PA team is very clear that their purpose is to help support businesses to make business and people decisions, and not to leverage individual data to make a particular call on one individual. They look for aggregated data, trends and patterns to understand what makes people thrive.

The company chose to put the entire employee life cycle processes onto one core HR data (SAP). They took a stand to integrate technologies to make those interface topics easier. They are also working with the concept of data lake. If an organisation has a variety of systems any-where and everywhere, it needs one common key among these to create one lake. Since the data are connected through one common key, it is possible to use it to do analytics.

Looking ahead, the company is building up as part of the journey. They believe the data are non-exhaustive, and they are putting considerable effort into predictive analytics and artificial intelligence. They believe they have surpassed the first stage of producing descriptive analytics and have moved into predictive analytics as a next step. They are helping HR and business leaders to model the future and to understand what are the few characteristics that can predict a specific phenomenon, so as to be able to anticipate events and take actions. Regarding artificial intelligence, by bringing tech-nology into play, they can augment the level of usage they can make from the data. The aim is to educate the business leaders to maximise the use of the data set as well as to have technology inform a business leader of an insight that they had not thought of.

In terms of process, the PA team's philosophy when tackling a problem is the following:

1. Always start with the hypothesis, with the business topic/question – What is the business trying to do? Why are they doing this (probing)? This is very important. They consciously do not start with the data because they know, from earlier experience, that it is easy to get lost in the data very quickly.
2. Next, break the problem down into sub-questions (sub-hypotheses).
3. Only then, go into the data, use the data to provide information and insights.

To ensure the data are accurate, the PA team has dedicated members that manage data. They check their completeness, accuracy, that they are updated and that they are not corrupted. This is done by cross-checking data against other systems. In addition, they have redefined processes and governance, so that they are moving away from data entry by HR only as much as possible and are getting employees to enter the data themselves. Data are usually the cleanest when they are entered at their source.

The PA team 1 believes that the key to success is to find out the 'Whys'. One example was their ability to innovate in many aspects of their three businesses: Healthcare, Life Sciences and Performance Materials. They realised that diversity was a trigger for innovation and that there was a sweet spot for diversity and helped use this insight as a strong input to define their people strategy. This was an eye-opener, especially for an engineering company, which is heavily innovation-driven, and where everyone has their own views about what drives innovation (Fig. 1.5).

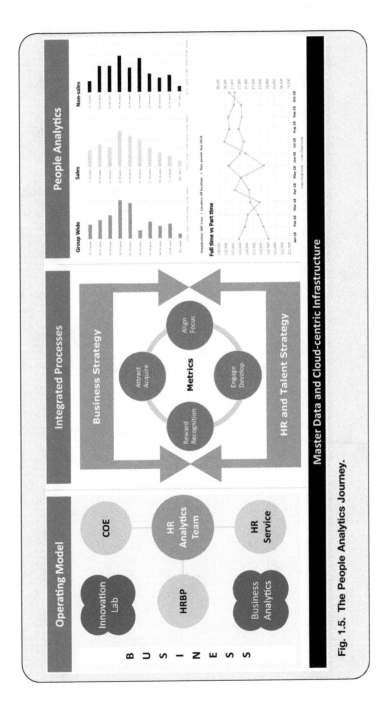

Fig. 1.5. The People Analytics Journey.

2

TOOLS FOR HR ANALYTICS

In this chapter, we seek to learn the components of analytics technology and understand the various technology options available.

First, we look at technology options, including on-premise and cloud-based. We take stock of issues related to the cost of implementing each type of solution. Next, we cover Software as a Service (SaaS).

The following section looks in more detail at the components of analytics technology, including Human Resource Information Systems (HRIS), HR data warehouses, reporting technology, statistical analysis and machine learning technology, visualisation technology and cognitive technology.

We conclude with a quick overview of two of the most popular tools for HR Analytics: Workday and Tableau.

2.1 TECHNOLOGY OPTIONS

A large part of the work in HR analytics involves the collection, clean-up and storage of data, and later, the ability to visualise the results of the analysis in a way that tells a convincing story. To assist in these, the analytics team must make use of a variety of technological tools. The sections below describe some of these tools. It is important to become familiar with at least some of them to make our work in HR analytics easier. At the same time, note that the existing technology is changing constantly, and new tools are also coming into being at an ever-increasing rate. Thus, it is important to stay informed about 'new and improved' technology options.

There are many other applications designed to make the work of HR easier, faster and more accurate, and that also helps to collect data (for instance, artificial intelligence applied to recruiting). However, generally the data still need to be processed elsewhere to derive answers to our questions. Hence, in this chapter, we only cover those tools that are important to conduct analytics projects.

2.1.1 On-premise

In our context, on-premise refers to solutions in the organisation's own data centre. That is to say, the software physically resides on the organisation's computers and servers, and inside of their firewall.

On-premise solutions are generally more customisable and offer greater control over data, but the upfront investment is greater. These solutions are usually priced under a one-time perpetual licence fee, with recurring fees for support, training and updates. Organisations also pay associated hardware and IT costs. In addition, on-premise solutions usually require ongoing servicing and maintenance from the internal IT team. Often, the IT team faces challenges in manipulating the existing on-premise solutions to support new applications or integrations.

2.1.2 Cloud Based

In a cloud-based environment, the software and data are hosted on the service provider's (remote) servers, and accessed through the Internet. Users have access to real-time data (anywhere, anytime!).

Cloud solutions require no upfront costs. They are priced under a subscription model, covering all maintenance, upgrades and other support services, with additional recurring fees for support, training and updates. This means that cloud solutions are cheaper up front, take less time to implement and are easier to use. As most things are taken care of by the service provider, the internal IT team typically focuses on IT strategy and aligning to business needs, rather than maintenance.

One of the key advantages of leveraging cloud solutions is that they offer organisations the flexibility to scale up (or down) – depending on the business needs and growth rate.

2.2 COST OF IMPLEMENTING ON-PREMISE VS CLOUD

Despite having ongoing subscription fees that can be increased or decreased depending on the scale that is needed, studies show (e.g. Hurwitz & Associates http://www.netsuite.com/portal/pdf/wp-hurwitztco-study-dynamics.pdf) that the total cost of ownership (TCO) – comprising capital expenses, operating expenses and indirect costs – for cloud is lower compared to on-premise.

Fig. 2.1 shows the potential costs (non-exhaustive) that are associated with the implementation of both systems. With these costs or expenses in mind, the Hurwitz & Associates study examines a sample of 100 users to determine the average cost incurred for cloud and on-premise. The results show that the total expense of installing and operating an on-premise system over four years was $1,400,570, almost twice that of a cloud solution, which totalled $697,656 over the same timeframe.

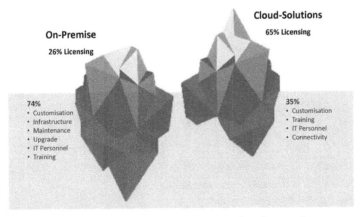

On-Premise

26% Licensing

Cloud-Solutions

65% Licensing

74%
- Customisation
- Infrastructure
- Maintenance
- Upgrade
- IT Personnel
- Training

35%
- Customisation
- Training
- IT Personnel
- Connectivity

Fig. 2.1. Total Costs of Ownership: Cloud-based vs On-premise.

2.3 SOFTWARE AS A SERVICE

Software as a service (SaaS) is a method of software delivery that allows data to be accessed from any device with an Internet connection and web browser. SaaS provides a complete software solution which organisations purchase on a pay-as-you-go basis from a cloud service provider. All the underlying infrastructure, middleware, application software and application data are located in the service provider's data centre. The service provider manages the hardware and software, within an appropriate service agreement, ensuring the availability and the security of the application as well as of the data.

Fig. 2.2 illustrates the concept of SaaS and other related concepts: Platform as a Service (PaaS) and Infrastructure as a Service (IaaS).

2.4 COMPONENTS OF ANALYTICS TECHNOLOGY

There are six distinct types of components of HR analytics, each with a different purpose. The analysts need to understand what sort of technology and tools to use in each case or each phase of their project.

The six components of analytics technology are:

1. HRIS

2. HR Data Warehouse

3. Reporting Technology

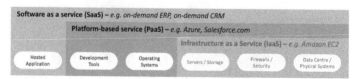

Source: 'What is SaaS?', Microsoft Azure.

Fig. 2.2. SaaS vs PaaS vs IaaS.

4. Statistical Analysis and Machine Learning Technology

5. Visualisation Technology

6. Cognitive Technology

Each is explained, in turn, as follows.

2.4.1 Human Resources Information System

At its core, an HRIS is a database to store employee information. All personnel data can be entered into the system, which can be accessed from anywhere, round the clock. Often, an HRIS also offers solutions for various HR sub-functions: payroll, benefits, learning, performance, recruiting, etc. Most are flexibly designed with integrated databases – comprehensive array of features, and reporting capabilities, that allows better workforce management.

The purposes of an HRIS include the ability to normalise the organisation's HR policies and practices into a workflow that reflects an organisation-wide view of best practices in HR. A good HRIS also provides the HR team with the capability to more effectively plan, control and manage HR costs.

An HRIS should allow for more accurate data collection, improved productivity of HR staff (by simplifying, among other things, the process of collecting resumes, automating time-off requests, etc.), resulting in faster approvals, less paperwork, and improved efficiency and quality in HR decision-making.

Oracle's PeopleSoft and SAP's SuccessFactors are commonly found HRIS systems. More recently, Workday has become widely used.

2.4.2 HR Data Warehouse

In simple terms, an HR data warehouse is a database that aggregates and rearranges historical talent data and other HR data, so that it is easy to query and analyse.

To have useful data, there is a need to link the data across various internal systems. To accomplish this end, it is important to take regular, periodic data exports from all relevant systems of record being used and to store the data in a specially constructed HR data warehouse. Data from operational systems are prepared in staging areas where data are cleansed and validated. Data are then transferred to an HR data warehouse. The HR data warehouse then becomes the master record. These data can later be used to populate other downstream systems that need accurate data for either advanced analytics or HR reporting purposes.

The HR data warehouse then would have HRIS data such as date of hire, salary, department, last performance appraisal score, etc. But it also contains cross-referenced data such as what is the engagement score of every department, the turnover rate of the country where each employee works, etc. So, for instance, to determine if the departments that have high turnover rate are also the ones with compa-ratio <1, all those data need to be in the HR data warehouse. Fig. 2.3 illustrates the structure of data systems of HR data warehouse.

2.4.3 Reporting Technology

A reporting tool typically sits over the top of the HRIS, HR data warehouses, or both. These also include business intelligence (BI) software applications.

Reporting applications allow users to undertake tasks such as querying HRIS for information about each of the HR

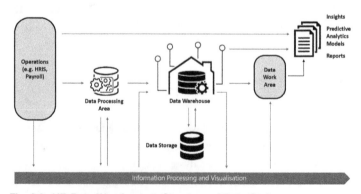

Fig. 2.3. HR Data Warehouse – Structure of Data Systems.

sub-functions – such as payroll reports, average time taken to fill vacancies, level of engagement with online learning systems, etc.

BI tools can support both strategic and tactical decision-making processes, by helping to identify business problems that need to be addressed. BI technology can also be used to examine how well the HR function is performing relative to a set of KPIs. This usually involves populating dashboards on HR metrics (e.g. turnover rates across business units/functions).

Most of the popular systems available – Workday, Tableau, PeopleSoft, Success Factors – have reporting tools. Excel can also be used as a reporting tool, since it allows creating graphs and charts.

2.4.4 Statistical Analysis and Machine Learning Technology

These technologies are used to test hypotheses. Data analysts rely on a range of software programmes, selecting a software package for the type of analysis they want to 'create' and 'calculate', or writing their own algorithms using open-source (such as R, Python) programming, or commercial software packages, which range from basic to advanced (such as Excel, SAS, SPSS).

These technologies can also include advanced data management systems – e.g. distributed computing used in Big Data platforms to share the computational burden of time-consuming data analysis across many computers.

Machine learning technology relies on artificial intelligence to create algorithms that learn from prior decisions and can thus build internal models that aid in making predictions on data. Ideally, these models are built from historical trends and relationships in the data to produce reliable predictions. Workday, for instance, has machine learning embedded in the software.

2.4.5 Visualisation Technology

Visualisation technology refers to software (such as Tableau) that can generate sophisticated graphs, and other visual representation of data. These tools help analysts to gain a clearer picture of the data they are considering and help those interpreting the data, so they can better understand the results of the analyses. One key aspect is that it makes it easier to convey the story to those who are less familiar with statistical jargon.

Visualisation technology also helps to reveal complex results. The more powerful tools can help to visualise data in 3D.

2.4.6 Cognitive Technology

This is a new area of technology based on artificial intelligence. This technology learns, reasons and advises HR users based on models that the system built and inferences that it makes. The users interact with the system using natural language and apply the models that the system builds.

According to a recent IBM report (https://www-01.ibm.com/common/ssi/cgi-bin/ssialias?htmlfid=GBE03789USEN), there are three areas in the HR domain that are most ready to take advantage of cognitive computing's capabilities – talent acquisition and onboarding, talent development and HR operations. Beyond these, there are several key areas where cognitive solutions are expected to have an impact:

- Highly complex decisions, requiring a wide variety of inputs from different data sources

- Frequent interactions by users – where large volumes of requests must be interpreted and addressed

- When high volumes of unstructured data are involved

- Personalised output to address the individual needs of a diverse workforce

SUMMARY

In this chapter, we have covered the following:

- Various technology options

- Components of analytics technology

We described various technology options including, on-premise, in the cloud, SaaS and their associated costs.

We then considered various available tools for HR analytics, focusing on HRIS, HR data warehouses, statistical, reporting and visualisation technologies, finishing with a brief look at machine learning, where the current developments for HR technology are proving to be very interesting.

The following sidebar delves into two of the more popular tools today: Tableau and Workday.

QUESTIONS

Below are a few key questions to ponder when considering the technology and tools for HR Analytics:

- Is software needed? Which? Are Excel and Tableau enough? What else is needed/useful?

- How about apps? There are certainly a good number of them out there. Are they needed/useful?

- What big data (vs small data) can be of use in HR analytics?

- Where to host the HR warehouse?

A Quick Overview of Tableau and Workday

Two of the more useful tools in HR analytics today are Tableau and Workday.

Tableau

Tableau is a powerful data visualisation tool that allows users to carry out calculations from existing data, drag and drop data elements and review statistics. One of the most useful features of Tableau for HR analytics is the ability to visually show trend analyses, regressions and correlations for ease of understanding. Tableau makes it easy to ask additional questions, spot trends, identify opportunities and evaluate hypotheses.

To read more and get an opportunity to demo this software, visit https://www.tableau.com/products/desktop.

Workday

Workday's Human Capital Management System aims to put together HR administration, workforce planning, recruiting and talent management into a single system to allow for overall visibility into the company's workforce.

Workday provides a comprehensive suite of applications to manage HR data. From an HR analytics point of view, two features stand out. One, of course, is the ability to house HR data in a single place. These data are related to Human Resource Management, People Analytics, Global Compliance, Audit and Internal Controls, Workforce Planning, Recruiting, Talent Management, Learning, Compensation, Benefits, Payroll Management and Time and Absence.

The second feature relates to the ability of the system to apply machine learning. This allows for better business decisions based on contextual insight. To get a hands-on demo on Workday for HR, visit https://www.workday.com/en-us/applications/human-capital-management.html.

3

DATA COLLECTION

Data collection involves finding valid and reliable data and making it useful for our analyses. This chapter aims to identify sources of data and data availability for HR analytics. In the main, we focus on 'small data' as few elements of HR Analytics deal with 'big data'.

Next, we explore common data quality challenges and how to overcome them: Missing data, outdated data, no data and outliers. In this context, we delve into data cleaning techniques and into considerations around checking data.

Finally, we consider exploratory data analysis as a necessary step to become comfortable with the data collected.

3.1 SOURCES OF DATA

There are plentiful sources of impactful data, whether hard or soft, big or small, for HR analytics. Below we list a number of sources, but note that there may be more:

3.1.1 HR Data

Not all HR data resides in the HR Information System (HRIS). In fact, many HR data are in other systems or, often, in no specific system. Some of these data can be found in the following:

- Payroll system

- Applicant tracking system (e.g. Taleo)

- Employee engagement surveys

- Executive remuneration data found in annual reports (Bussin & Diez, 2016)

3.1.2 HRIS Data

There are many types of HRIS (e.g. SAP, Workday, PeopleSoft), and they can be either on-premise or in the cloud. The usual design is as a database with similar capabilities involving data entry, data tracking and data information needs for HR, payroll and talent management. Key functionalities include the following:

- Management of basic employee information: name, title, gender, address, etc.

- Benefits management, including enrolment, personal information, updates, leave management, etc.

- Payroll integration, including variable pay, overtime, allowances, etc.

- Applicant tracking, resume management and integration with employee information if a candidate is hired. This includes matching offer letters with the salary administration data and with payroll.

- Performance management, including pay for performance and linkages to payroll

- Training history, including certifications, licences, individual development plans, etc.

- Succession planning, including high potential identification, where the employee could be posted next, others ready to take his or her role and risk assessment. Other assessments could be stored here.

- Information about the employee worth storing such as awards, commendations, disciplinary actions, etc. attendance, pay history, positions held at the company, etc.

3.1.3 Non-HR Data

This can, of course, mean anything! But mainly we focus on how HR can impact business results, and thus we concentrate on business-related data, such as follows:

- **Finance:** Revenue, profits, costs

- **Marketing:** Customer satisfaction, customer retention

- **Operations:** Defect rates, returned goods

In fact, most of the impact measures we can use for HR analytics that relate HR to business results are readily available in databases or systems somewhere in the organisation.

3.1.4 Data Audits

A data audit is a useful process to assess the quality of your data. For our purposes, 'quality' is measured by the following:

- Accuracy across all systems

- Completeness in a timely manner

- Consistency and adherence to business rules

- Availability accessibility and appropriate security

Regular audits of all data systems should be completed to ensure that:

- When the data are used for analytics, there is one source of truth of the information to be used

- The data can be easily accessed in a timely manner

- The data are not questioned when used for analytics.

Do the data need to be 100% accurate? In practice, we can work with different levels of accuracy and confidence needed for different sources of data. For example,

- Headcount? Probably needs to be accurate (as far as possible) as it is the basis of many other measures and could become a main cause of dispute

- Leaver reason? Does not need to be 100% accurate, but more of a directional trend. If 20% or 23% of people left because of career opportunities, the decisions you make will not likely change.

3.1.5 Structured and Unstructured Data

Traditional data sources capture the past but are not always the best source of data to understand the current state. Usually, traditional data tend to be structured – it fits into established categories. These data tend to be static (minor changes over time) and are updated infrequently.

New data sources can be a constant stream of real-time, unstructured (open text) data. This can be very useful and exciting, but caution must be taken as data may fluctuate in response to changes within the environment. Integrating structured and unstructured data increases the power of analytics. We list some examples as follows:

- Email Traffic. Headers and calendars data could be useful to track behavioural patterns and movement in the workspace. Who writes to whom, and who is been written to in the 'To' or in the 'CC' line, can help detect informal networks, link behaviour and help with the optimal design of organisation, work and physical space, and provide feedback and coaching to individuals. Email traffic can also help determine productivity or forecast the ability to deliver projects on time.

- Electronic Sensing Badges. These can help to analyse internal social networks, interaction patterns, time allocations and demands made on others' time. It can then provide an aggregated analysis to company and give individuals confidential feedback.

- Enterprise Social Platforms. The data from these can help to identify emerging issues, map hotspots, and thus determine where pre-emptive actions can reduce negative outcomes (turnover, drop in engagement, etc.). The data can also be used to track results of managerial actions and, ultimately, to find expertise within the organisation.

- CCTV. Face recognition software allows you to track people flow. For example, you can track the time people arrive and leave, how often they take breaks, the number of people that go to training and stay throughout, etc.

Big data, for HR analytics, refers to data outside of the organisation which can be sourced from the Internet, regardless of the size of the data. For example, census data offer an opportunity for HR to identify potential candidates by geography. Often, HR can link to marketing or other areas of business analytics to share some of the data they have collected. For instance, liking consumer trends to training needs.

HR data will work to give you HR answers to HR questions. For instance, if you want to know if turnover is a function of pay, years in service or time since last promoted, you can get an answer with HR data. But if you want to know the relationship between turnover and profits, you need financial data. Or it could be that you may want to know the relationship between turnover and customer satisfaction. To do this you need marketing data to show that customer satisfaction is related to profits; if you can find that there is a relationship between customer satisfaction and turnover then, by transitivity, you now know there's a relationship between turnover and profits. You could also look at manufacturing data, for instance, to find if the training that you are providing to your employees on the line translates into better quality products.

Data generally sit in various places, but you want it to be in a single place to make analytics easier. This idea of the data sitting all in one place is your data warehouse.

3.2 COMMON DATA CHALLENGES AND SOLUTIONS

There are a variety of problems we can encounter with managing data. Here we will mention four of them; First is missing data, second is old data, third is no data, the fourth is outliers.

3.2.1 Missing Data

Missing data challenge is common; The first problem with missing data is when you try to guess to fill it. This is easier to do if you're only missing a few data points, but if you're missing many data points, it will get complicated. If you have some idea of the overall compensation of your population, you may make reasonable guesses. But every time you do this, you could run into trouble. What you're trying to do in attempting to complete the data is to determine the way in which you will cause the least damage. The steps below provide an approach to do so:

Step 1: Determine the cause of missing value: Can the data set be used?

- Random reasons or,
  - E.g. data entry errors
- Reasons related to the topic of study
  - E.g. participants intentionally skip answering the question
- Ignoring missing data may lead to incorrect conclusions

Step 2: Verify if analysis should proceed

Step 3: Determine the best approach to address missing values

Some possible solutions are as follows:

- Eliminate cases with missing values from analysis (Cons: reduces the representativeness of the sample – could possibly cause biased results)
- Replace missing cases with estimation – using appropriate assumptions or modelling techniques (e.g. regression equations)

Example:

Participants	Gender
001	F
002	F
003	
004	M
005	F
006	M
007	
008	M
009	F

3.2.2 Outdated Data

When you have old data, you basically go through the same process as with missing data. That is to say, if you have a trend and have an idea of how the trend looks, you can make a reasonable estimate going forward. Often, you can make educated guesses. However, sometimes, you can make big mistakes by doing this. Sometimes, it is better to wait for better data. This happens often with salary surveys; Do you wait until the annual increases are provided, or do you use old data and assume an increase?

Some judgement is needed to determine how much of an issue it is for the analysis and conclusions.

- If the **number of outdated values is large** enough to influence the outcome of the analysis, it is best to obtain updated information

- Can use **Sensitivity Analysis** (a technique to determine how different values of an independent variable impact a particular dependent variable under given assumptions) to determine if the outdated values are large enough to affect the outcome

- If data refresh cycles are frequent, may wait for the next refresh. Otherwise, consider obtaining data from a different source and merge with the master data set.

An example: You want to determine if compensation is related to productivity. In order to perform this analysis, you would need to extract data from HRIS. But you've learnt that the data set does not reflect recent off-cycle salary increment because the compensation system has yet to synchronise with the core system.

- **Solution Option 1**: Find the specific update schedule and determine if it is possible to wait for a data refresh

- **Solution Option 2**: Extract data manually from the payroll system and merge it with the master data (HRIS extraction)

3.2.3 No Data Available

Another common problem is data availability. Without data it is difficult to do any modelling. In general, if this is the situation, it is at least possible to come up with potential hypotheses and start collecting data moving forward, so that you can make better inferences in the future. This is normally useful in cases of assessments or recruiting. It is feasible to create the assessment tests first and do assessments of the people currently in the company. With that data, going forward, the potential hires should answer the questions in a similar way as those who are already in the company. Thus, slowly build on the hypotheses. Without data, one must tread very careful with assumptions. Proxies can be used sometimes – internal or external. In every case, you are trying to come up with bad data. It is useable but must be used carefully.

An example: You want to determine the cause of high attrition. You have several factors to consider but the line manager insists that the fault lies in the promotion history – which is not recorded in the system. Does lack of data mean you cannot consider this variable in your analysis?

- **Possible Solution 1:** Approximate data by using a combination of variables that currently exist in the database; e.g. look for instances where employees had a title change and a corresponding salary change.

- **Possible Solution 2:** Consider external publicly available data as a proxy; e.g. job title changes posted on LinkedIn.

3.2.4 Data Outliers

The fourth issue is outliers. Outliers are values that are abnormally higher or lower than most other values in a sample of data. It is important to identify outliers as just a few extreme values may alter the results considerably.

In looking at a graphical representation of the data, it appears that some points do not align with the rest. Should these data points be included or not? First thing is to double-check if there was any data input error, if the data are real. If the data are real, do we automatically assume they're outliers? Sometimes, outliers are legitimate values; other times, they are a result of a data entry error. If it is the former, we go with the data given. It might give an odd, but perhaps right model. If it is the latter, that can be easily fixed by consulting the data owners to help determine what the right number should be.

How do we know if any one point is truly an outlier? The best approach is to make a probabilistic analysis.

Step 1: Examine the distribution of data prior to statistical analysis. A graphical representation usually works well, as can be seen in the example below:

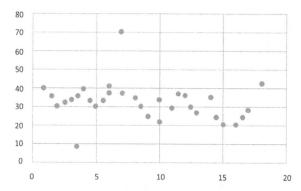

Step 2: As a rule of thumb, any data point that lies +/− three standard deviations away from the mean of your data is likely to be an outlier. In a normal distribution, the probability that any point in the data sample will fall three standard deviations away from the mean is 99%. Thus, any data point that falls +/− three standard deviations from the mean only has a 1% probability or less of being in any other sample that you may do in the future. It is possible then to confidently get rid of the outlier because it is unlikely to occur again.

It is worth noting that, in the day-to-day work of HR analytics, the normal bell curve (the S-curve) hardly ever happens. Bell curves are found more often in naturally occurring things, such as height, weight, amount of rainfall, amount of sunshine, etc. The things we deal with in HR analytics – pay rates, turnover rates, performance appraisals, even intelligence – will not follow a normal distribution. The main reason is that HR processes are usually biased, from a statistical point of view. The data are generally skewed because we set it out to be skewed. We hardly do anything that would follow a random pattern – we hire people that we think are smart, we promote people who are more capable; we slow down pay increases over time. Most everything we do is going to be skewed. However, for purposes of determining outliers, the three-standard-deviation rule of thumb is nonetheless useful.

3.3 TIDYING THE DATA

Tidying the data refers to the work of converting the data from raw form to directly analysable form prior to any data analysis. For instance, you have to clean up the data so they all are in the same units. A common example is, when comparing salaries across countries, to make sure they are in the same currency. When comparing male and female employees, sometimes the data come as 'M' and 'F' so, you need to set the coding to a numeric value which is applied consistently and can be used for modelling: '1' for Males and '2' for Females, for example. Another example is cleaning the data for consistency. When looking at performance ratings, is '1' or '5' the highest or the lowest rating? Keep track of what changes were made when tidying data, so in future others will know what you did.

3.3.1 General Principles of Tidy Data

There are some useful guidelines to remember when tidying data. Below are some of them:

- **Each variable you measure should be in one column;** don't mix them up in the data set. For instance, 'High Performance' in one column, 'High Pay' in another column. You can mix them later in a third column, or when you do your actual calculation, but best to keep all three columns in your data set; otherwise, if you only use the blended column, you will not be able to separate them later.

- **Place each different observation of a variable in a different row.** In an Excel database, each item (your data) should be in a column, and each observation that you have, should be in a row. This will help with the analysis, modelling and data visualisation later.

- **Have only one table for each 'kind' of variable;** say, an analysis of employee performance in one table, and an analysis of employee pay in another table.

- **When you have multiple tables, each should include a column that allows them to be linked.** In the above-mentioned example, to look at the relationship between performance and pay, you need to have a way to link the two. Ideally, there is one column, your identifier column, that allows to keep track of data across sheets; in this case, 'employee number' could work.

- **Include a row at the top of each data table/spreadsheet that contains each row's full name.** It is good practice to label everything properly, so when you return to your work, you can make sense of the data; or when you leave the company, the next person can make sense of the data.

In summary, a processed data set should include:

- The rawest form of the data

- A tidy data set

- A code book describing each variable and its values in the tidy data set

- An explicit and exact recipe you used to go from 1 to 2; Reproducibility is key

Remember than even with a tidy data set, processing is required to make it slightly easier to analyse or use the data for modelling.

3.3.2 Common Mistakes When Tidying Data

- **Combining multiple variables into a single column:** Making one column represent two variables, for example, combining gender and age range into a single variable

- **Merging unrelated data into a single file:** If you have measurements on very different topics, for example, a person's finances and their health, it is often a better idea to save each one as a different table with a common unique identifier

- **An instruction list that is not explicit:** When an instruction list that is not a computer script is used, a common mistake is to not report the parameters or versions of software used to perform an analysis

3.3.3 Tips on Checking Data

- **Interactive analysis is the best way to explore data.** Make plots and tables, identify quirks, outliers, missing data patterns and problems with the data.

- **Avoid coding categorical or ordinal variables as numbers:** This will avoid potential mix-ups about which direction effects go and will help identify coding errors

- **Always encode every piece of information about your observations using text:** Rather than highlighting certain data points as questionable, you should include an additional column that indicates which measurements are questionable and which are not

- **Identify the missing value indicator:** You should use a single common code for all missing values (for example, 'NA'), rather than leaving any entries blank

- **Check for clear coding errors:** It is common for variables to be miscoded. The first step is to determine whether these are missing values, miscoding or whether the scale was incorrectly communicated

- **Check for label switching:** When data on the same individuals are stored in multiple tables, a very common error is to have mislabelled data. The best way to detect these mislabelling is to look for logical inconsistencies

- **If you have data in multiple files, ensure that data that should be identical across files is identical:** In some cases, you will have the same measurements recorded twice. For example, you may have the gender of a patient recorded in two separate data tables

- **Check the units (or lack of units):** It is important to check that all variables have values on the unit scale you expect. Histograms and boxplots are good ways to check that the measurements you observe fall on the right scale.

- **Plot as much of the actual data** as you can. Plotting more of the data allows you to identify outliers, confounders, missing data, relationships and correlations much more easily than with summary measures.

- **'Spread out' data** with varying orders of magnitude. Data measured across multiple scales will often be highly skewed, with many values near zero. One way to 'spread the values out' is to take the log transform of the data. Taking the log of ratio-valued data will often make the distribution more symmetric. Since the log of one is also zero, values of zero on the log scale can be interpreted as equality of the two values in the ratio.

3.3.4 Common Mistakes When Checking the Data

- **Failing to check the data at all:** A common temptation in data analysis is to load the data and immediately leap to statistical modelling. Checking the data before analysis is a critical step in the process

- **A common source of error is data entry:** As much as possible, data should be downloaded directly. Even then, do not assume it's correct. A good way to check is to do random checks, like checking every 10th item of data, to make sure it is clean.

- **Encoding factors as quantitative numbers:** If a scale is qualitative, but the variable is encoded as 1, 2, 3, etc., then statistical modelling functions may interpret this variable as a quantitative variable and incorrectly order the values

- **Not making sufficient plots:** A common mistake is to only make tabular summaries of the data when doing data checking. When data are plotted in a graph, it makes it easier to see odd data/outliers. Creating a broad range of data visualisations, one for each potential problem in a data set, is an effective way to identify problems

- **Failing to look for outliers or missing values:** A common mistake is to assume that all measurements follow the appropriate distribution. Plots of the distribution of the data for each measured variable can help to identify outliers. If you don't look for the outliers, you may not know there's a problem.

When managing big (or even small!) data warehouses, it is good practice to have data checking routines going on all the time. For instance, HR consultancies that develop salary surveys typically set standards of +/− three standard deviations against the prior year's data for consistency, missing data, and just to make sure the data looks like what it's supposed to. One question frequently tested against is whether there is a job code for which this year's salary is lower than last year's. If so, what made the data go down? It could be that several of last year's incumbents are no longer on the job, and this year's incumbents have a lower salary. Understanding what happened helps users of the information to gain trust in the data analysis.

3.3.5 Plots Are Better than Summaries

You can explore data by calculating summary statistics, for example the correlation between variables. However, in the examples below, all these data sets have the exact same correlation and regression line, which would not be helpful in these cases.

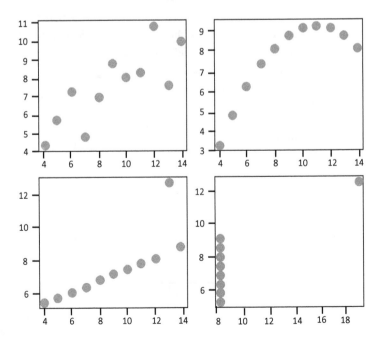

Using colour/size to check for confounding is another good practice. When plotting the relationship between two variables on a scatterplot, you can use the colour or size of points to check for a confounding relationship. For example, in this plot it looks like the more you study, the worse score you get on the test:

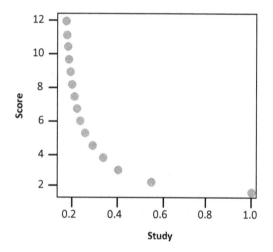

...but if you size the points by the skill of the student, you see that more skilled students don't study as much. So, it is likely that skill is confounding the relationship.

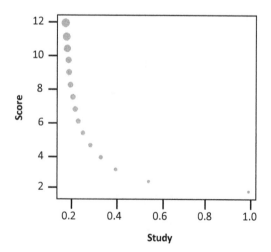

The goal is to quickly understand a data set; during exploratory data analysis speed is more important than style. Any strong pattern in a data set should be checked for confounders and alternative explanations. Look particularly for patterns of missing values and the impact they might have on conclusions. Missing data are often simply ignored by statistical software, but this means that if the missing data have informative patterns, then analyses will ultimately be biased. Avoid the urge to jump too quickly into statistical tests.

The end objective is to 'massage' and 'play' with the data to become very familiar with it. As an HR professional, a 'moment of truth' occurs when you get in front of an audience of line managers and explain, for instance, that the main reason for turnover in the company is not related to pay, but to poor leadership. You are telling this to the managers whom, in effect, just heard you call them 'bad'. When you look at the situation from their perspective, their assumptions may be: 'You're from HR. We think HR is at fault in this turnover problem. But of course, you're going to stand here and tell us it is not HR at fault. And of course, you're going to say management is at fault. Therefore, whatever you're telling me, I'm not going to believe you'. But they will only think this. What they'll say instead is: 'It must be pay; did you check for pay?' So, you say that, of course, you checked for pay; and it turns out the correlation between pay and turnover that you calculated using three years of company-specific data is only 0.17, whereas the correlation between turnover and bad management is 0.82. Then, they're likely to say, 'Your pay data must be wrong'. This is exactly when you need to know your pay data really well. This is when you need to demonstrate that you have looked at the data in many different ways, you checked, thoroughly, you found two errors and fixed them. You are 100% sure these data are right. Then, and only then, will the line managers actually consider the possibility that lack of leadership is a bigger problem with regards to turnover in the company.

There's no substitute for knowing your data really well. Plot the data. Look at the data. Get a sense of what's happening with the data. Start making sense of the data. Then you can make hypotheses.

SUMMARY

In this session, we have covered the following:

- The common data quality challenges and approach to overcome the challenges

- Data cleaning techniques

- Data checking methodology

- Overview of exploratory data analysis.

QUESTIONS

Practice searching for data in the Internet that could be useful in HR analytics.

For instance, look for the following:

- Your client is seeking your advice on the attractiveness to relocate workers to Malaysia

- Your CHRO would like to know what the estimated time to proficiency for an actuary is

- Your client would like to know the future labour availability for oral health therapists in Singapore

- Your client would like to know the labour supply of speech therapists in Singapore

- English proficiency is an important recruiting criterion for your client; they are not able to decide if they should recruit from Indonesia or Thailand

- Your client would like to find out more about the labour quality of engineers in India

CASELET

A bank wanted to study what were the HR drivers of branch profitability. They had collected data on branch revenue, derived from all of the accounts that are captured, as well as interest on loans and credit cards that they had granted. They also had data on branch costs, including the monies paid out as interest on deposits; they also had data on the payroll costs for the people who work at each branch, both full-time and part-time, plus other expenses such as office rent and overheads. Some of the branches were more profitable than others.

From a people standpoint, what could be some causes of revenue and profit? Below are some of the hypotheses the HR team considered:

- Good teamwork generates people effectiveness and productivity and thus lower cost and higher revenue

- Greater diversity (Hypothesis: Diverse teams generate more profit)

- Competency – The higher the skills set available at the branch, the higher the profit

- Training – fintech training (Hypothesis: More hours of training translates into more profit. For those that need training, provide training)

- Higher pay mix; the higher the variable pay in the mix, the higher the profit

- Average years of experience (Hypothesis: The more experience, the higher the profit)

- High branch turnover leads to low profitability

Armed with this list of hypotheses that they believe in (up to a point), they realised that these were biased. A comment from the HR Business Partner summarises it: 'As we are HR people, we only think of HR things'. They decided to speak to the business folks, and learnt that their hypotheses of people drivers of profitability had to do with the following:

- Attitude, meaning more willingness to work hard and, as a result, achieve better profitability.

- Similarly, the line thought more hours worked meant more profits.

- Employee's experience in other banks also meant, in the line manager's view, that they would be able to achieve better results.

Next, they spoke to the employees to get their perspective. From their view, profitability was a function of:

- How far is the branch from their home? (Hypothesis: the further I live from the branch, the less likely I am to work overtime, the lower the profit)

- Hours of training received had a positive impact on profits

- Quality of the manager (Hypothesis: the better the manager, the higher the engagement, the bigger the profit)

Thus, they had a very comprehensive list of hypotheses, derived from many stakeholders' points of view. Next, they started testing each hypothesis, one by one. In doing so, they learnt a few things. For instance, to test for distance from home vs profits they realised they needed two variables – one is distance from home, second is hours of work. However, as they dug deeper into the numbers, they noticed this was not enough as they had not made the connection between hours worked and profitability. At this point, they carried out statistical analysis of the data to figure which of these variables were correlated to which of other variables. This would allow them to only pick the ones that were truly needed to be correlated to these. They did not need to look at everything. For example, they already knew the hours worked were linked to distance from home. They also realised that hours worked were also a function of whether the (more so female) employee had children, and whether or not they drove to work in their own car. Then they established that the hours worked were indeed correlated with profitability. Once they learn these facts, they only needed to check hours worked because the other variables were really just partial explanations of this main hypothesis.

Subsequently, they carried out a multiple regression. This allowed them to determine the importance (weight) of each of the variables studied, and a model that explained over 70% of the variances. Then, from that model, they decided which variables to focus on in terms of changes to HR policies that would make a difference in achieving greater profitability.

Finally, they ended up with a set of meaningful variables. That set of variables made up a 'Talent Scorecard' for each branch manager to monitor. The scorecards tracked the variables they had found helped to explain HR's impact on branch profitability, to a certain degree (as we're never 100% confident), as well as the difference made (in the variables and in profitability) by the HR programs implemented to address them. For instance, they had found that at least 40 hours of training in new products made a difference, and that there was no difference after 80 hours of training. Thus, they ensured all employees received at least 40 hours, but not more than 80 hours of training, and the scorecard tracked this.

This caselet illustrates the importance of starting the analytical process with the business strategy (e.g. increase branch profitability). Then, develop hypotheses that link (measurable and aligned) HR variables and branch profits. These are tested to determine the strength of the relationship. From there, it is possible to move to impact.

It is important to note that benchmarking subject is not the same as analytics. Let's take turnover as an example: Just because a certain amount of turnover is an industry norm, it does not mean that if your company is below this number, it is good enough. For example, the company requires a particular type of engineer that has a specific set of skills important for achieving product quality. Even if average runover is less than industry norm, it may be that the company has a harder time replacing these engineers, as opposed to the rest of the industry, because of the characteristics it is looking to hire. To this company, turnover may be a bigger problem than to the industry. Just because average turnover rate is in line with the industry, and therefore they assume they are ok, does not really address how profitability is tied to turnover for the company. That would be akin to passing benchmarking off as analytics. However, if the company had done the analysis to understand the relationship between turnover and profits, it would be understandable if they then used benchmarking as a reference check.

4

HR ANALYTICS MODELLING

In this chapter we will delve deeper into the analytics design framework to better understand how to apply it when faced with HR analytics questions. In particular, we will introduce the data analysis question-type flow chart, which is a helpful tool to identify how best to tackle specific problems. We will also introduce readers to model building, which is an essential skill for HR analysts. Finally, we will learn more about supervised and unsupervised methods.

4.1 DETAILS OF ANALYTICS DESIGN FRAMEWORK

4.1.1 Source of Problem or Opportunity

The core idea behind modelling is to look at a set of data or at a graph and come up with ideas on what could be happening that might explain the data or the patterns in the graph. In short, it is akin to coming up with hypotheses, and then deciding on what to do with them.

Usually, when faced with a prospective HR analytics problem, the process is more or less like this: Someone 'sees' a problem – it could be the line people, the employees, someone from HR, etc. – and comes up with a question or a problem statement. This could be something like 'we hire people, and within a year many of them leave; why is that?' Or perhaps 'despite the fact that we hire more women than men, we have a majority of males on our senior rank.'

In a world without data or analytics, people would have to come up with 'educated guesses' to explain why the patterns look so. If no one else can come up with a better 'educated guess', then the explanation provided becomes true because nobody else has data to argue against it. However, if alternative 'educated guesses' are provided, then we have no clear way to decide, and often votes are 'weighed' rather than counted.

What we want to do with HR analytics is to get away from this idea that an 'educated guess' in HR is pitted against another 'educated guess' from a line executive, by making everything data-based. Take, for example, a discussion that goes something along the lines of: 'Google gives its employees free steaks at lunchtime, and their employee turnover rate is lower than 5%, so maybe we should give our employees steaks too, and our turnover rate would go down'. This is often the problem with benchmarking against best practices, that we take something like Google's steaks completely out of context, and it, all of a sudden, appears to make sense. This is when we need analytics to help figure out if this idea is really true.

Another typical example is a situation when perhaps someone in the HR team read an article or attended a conference where a consultant floated an idea that could potentially benefit your company. The specific piece of research quoted made specific reference that the practice in question was implemented in America, and they implied that it should work everywhere else. However, when the idea, and its source, is aired at the company, the typical reaction is: 'This is not the United States; it may work there for the big multi-nationals but not in our emerging market'. This type of argument is something we can often easily put to the test. It is important to validate if whatever others are selling us as the truth will work in a specific market, simply because it has been done and researched somewhere else.

One aspect of HR which can be much more data-driven relates to proper benchmarking of practices in other companies that are more or less similar to yours. Let us say that, for instance, companies in your industry have average sales per salesperson of $1 million, but yours is only $800,000. On learning that piece of information, what conclusions can be drawn? Is the company hiring the wrong people? Is it setting the wrong targets? Is it that incentives are not well positioned? Or that price is different than the competitors' price? It could be any one of those, or none or a combination. Proper benchmarking should provide a piece of information that can be tested.

Another source could be that we want to forecast the future as it links to manpower planning. For instance, in social services, some countries are faced with a population that is aging rapidly. In Singapore, for example, with a local population of around 3.5 million and growing at less than 1.2%, the government is forecasting that, by 2030, about a quarter of the local population (around 900,000 citizens) will be over the age of 65 years. This has implications on healthcare, housing, mental health, the need for home nursing, the demand for physical therapists and occupational therapists, gerontologists and perhaps even clinical psychologists. From a HR analytics point of view, we can help determine how many more physical therapists are needed by hypothesising that there is a correlation between the amount of people over the age of 65 years, over the age of 70 years, over the age of 80 years and over the age of 90 years, and the amount of incidences that probabilistically can occur where therapists – or any of the other professions – are needed. From there, actions can be taken to increase the number of graduates, retain more professionals, increase the conversion programmes, etc. Analytics can help figure out if the targets for service can be met.

Even 'experience' can be enhanced with analytics. Sometimes you may hear: 'we have done this before and it worked', but do we know why? For instance, a talent acquisition head can claim to have changed the recruitment process and the people recruited were better as a consequence. But, can we understand what is it that made it better? How to help the head of sales understand why is it that this particular group of salespeople can consistently sell 20%–30% more than the average salesperson? What is it that this person is, has or does that can help explain it? Answers to these questions can lead the organisation to decide if it should hire more people with these characteristics, or instead train more people in this particular way, so that sales can go up.

And sometimes, it can be sheer curiosity! Are graduates from one university more likely to leave the company within three years than those from other universities? Is distance from work a predictor of turnover? Or distance between the children's school and work a better predictor? There is a famous example from Google where they even studied ideally how long the lines at the company cafeteria should be in order to promote internal networking.

The possibilities are endless, once you start down this path, as long as you keep the end in mind; that is, will we learn something that is actionable and has a positive return.

All of these are possible ways in which problems can show up at the HR analyst desk. None of them is better than any other one. Although, from the point of view of management, there are two that they care about more: one is when they ask the HR analyst to go help answer nagging problems. These are usually to help resolve a long-standing issue that has been debated without resolution. Reasons for turnover, causes of low engagement scores, quick exits can fall into this category although there could be many others, even non-HR-related, questions. The second type are insightful ideas from the HR analytics team that can help the company make or save money.

Fig. 4.1 summarises these sources of problems or opportunities.

Fig. 4.1. Summary of Sources of Problems or Opportunities.

4.1.2 Scoping the Project

Once there is clarity about the kind of problem to be addressed, the next step is to determine how to tackle it. How to turn the problem into something we can analyse and for which we can find answers. We need to translate a problem or opportunity into objectives and requirements from a business perspective. A good approach to accomplish this is to scope the project by outlining the 'Context', 'Need', 'Vision' and 'Outcome'.

Context means defining clearly what is it that we are trying to find out, what is it that we are solving for. The more we can write a statement like this in business terms, the better. For instance, scoping a project as: 'we are trying to reduce turnover rate', can be scoped as: 'we want to increase people-related productivity'. It may seem subtle, but the latter is more aligned to the business outcome than the former, and gives a different scope to the problem at hand. If scoped as turnover rate, that becomes the 'y', or dependent variable, the one we are solving for; and yet we don't know if turnover rate and business results are correlated, what the direction of causality is and to what degree, If scoped as productivity, it becomes the 'y' variable, and the business is more likely to support it. To illustrate this point with another example, imagine a company that is concerned with low levels of engagement and how these affect the already high turnover rate. Should the problem statement be phrased as: 'We want to increase retention', or as 'We want to increase engagement scores'? The data that are needed to look at these two problem statements are likely to be different in each case. If the company wants to increase engagement scores, it may just look at the variables in the engagement survey index and only address those variables. Whereas if the problem is scoped as increasing retention, the HR analyst may want to look at other items that may not be in the engagement survey, such as distance from home, how long since the last promotion, did the employee recently marry, did they recently have a baby, how old are the employee's parents, how long since the employee graduated with an undergraduate degree, from which university and with what grades? Has the employee recently updated their LinkedIn profile? Have they been away from work intermittently lately? The important part of this exposition is that the way the problem is defined also defines the 'y' variable and, as a consequence, the 'x', or independent variables that will go into the model. If the scope is constrained at the beginning, it may not be possible to tackle the full extent of the problem.

There are other issues that need to be addressed at this stage: who are the stakeholders, who is likely to be supportive, who are the people who will not be happy with what you may find out? At this point it is also important to be aware of the constraints that may be in place: are the data readily available (and relatively clean!)? By when is this answer needed? How much money can be thrown at it (it will help determine how many people can work on the project, or if contract help will be available, etc).

The second part involved in scoping is *need*. The questions addressed in this step relate to what it is that analytics can bring to the table that cannot be easily done in any other way. The objective is to be able to demonstrate that analytics can provide a detailed answer, a thorough answer, an unquestionable answer, an answer that will help end the discussion on the topic and to guide actions in the right direction. More often than not, when faced with a problem or opportunity, there will be different anecdotes and opinions from various parts and levels in the organisation which will be used as if it was 'data' and will differ from each other. Analytics then becomes a tool to resolve the existing conflict.

Continuing with the example above about enhancing productivity by reducing turnover, what this step helps achieve is the need for analytics as a way to answer the question objectively and thoroughly. By setting out to look at as many variables as possible within the problem statement, there is a real opportunity to settle old – and conflicting – opinions once and for all. It is important to let all stakeholders know how they will benefit from analytics. Particularly if the project is likely to provide insights that were not known before, such as the impact of distance from home to work on turnover rate, when coupled with other variables such as age of parents or of children, for example.

The third part of this approach is *vision*. What would the answer look like if data, time and resources were available? Ideally all stakeholders will be able to visualise what the answer to this problem will give them.

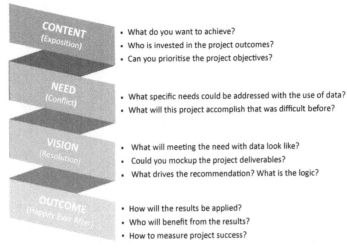

Fig. 4.2. Summary of Scoping Approach.

The *outcome* is that, when the problem is solved and the solution is found, the problem will be resolved and actions can be taken to address it. But beware, analytics usually has a dark side: not every problem can be solved using analytics. Before crunching any data, it is best to have clarity in what is it that needs to be done, what is it that you're solving for, what will it take to get there and how are these data going to be used. In particular, be sure that the issue is important enough (how much money can be made or saved if I know the answer to this question?) to warrant solving it. So, best to put the possible solution in this context. Fig. 4.2 summarises these points regarding scoping of problems or opportunities.

Once scoped, a needs analysis should be conducted to make the case to proceed:

- What intangible benefits are important?

- How can we fund the project?

- Is this issue critical?

- It is possible/feasible to correct it?

- How much is it costing the organisation?

- Are multiple solutions available?

- What happens if we do nothing?

- How much will the solution(s) cost?

- Is this issue linked to strategy?

- What is the potential payoff (ROI)?

4.1.3 Linking HR Variables to Business Measures

Data analysts often talk about the concept of big data. Big data is usually thought of as large data sets that can be mined to look for trends or patterns that help to understand relationships between various inputs and outcomes. For our purposes, we can define 'Big Data' as data that are outside of the organisation. And we can also define the concept of 'Small Data' as data that you already have, or can create, inside the organisation.

Most HR problems that HR analysts will tackle, with rare exceptions that use job portal, economic, census data or education data, deal only with internal data (i.e. small data). Small data can also be understood as being of two types: hard data and soft data. Hard data are generally found in operations systems, accounting systems and the like; they are data linked to facts that can be readily measured and understood. It could be cases of product sold in a day, revenue from services provided by a consulting form or expenses per claim of the claims processed in the last quarter at an insurance company.

Fig. 4.3 provides a detailed summary of hard and soft data. To understand this table, it is worthwhile to look at it closely. Look, for instance, at the quality column. One definition of quality revolves around the probability of errors in a manufacturing process (note that the same idea can be used for the number of bad hires in a recruiting process). Motorola developed the idea of Six Sigma as a tool for improving manufacturing processes to a standard which will yield a probability of defects-free products of no more than six standard deviations from the mean (99.99966%) defect-free, meaning the organisation is willing to

HARD DATA				SOFT DATA			
Volume	Quality	Cost	Time	Customer Service	Work Satisfaction	Employee Growth	A challenge with soft data versus hard data is converting soft measures to monetary values
Completion rate	Dropout rate	Variable costs	Time to proficiency	Loyalty	Engagement	Promotions	
Applications rejected	Shortages	Fixed costs	Equipment downtime	Complaints	Loyalty	Capability	
Productivity	Incidents	Operating costs	Cycle time	Retention	Stress	Networking	
Items sold	Error rate	Overhead costs	Time to completion	Lost customers	Burnout rate	Programs completed	
Patients attended	Product defects	Expenses	Lead time	Impressions	Grievances	Request for transfer	

Fig. 4.3. Examples of Hard and Soft Data.

tolerate 3.4 defective parts per million. However, achieving this standard is not always true for all companies or all products. For instance, let's say you are a semiconductor company that manufactures the chips that open the airbags in cars when they are involved in a crash. You would not want to run the risk that, 3.4 times in a million, one of those bags did not open. Each time a bag fails to open, someone can be seriously injured, or worse. In such cases, you would aim at zero defects. Other products are more susceptible to be acceptable even at a level of defects higher than six sigma, as it may be more costly to achieve higher levels of quality than to replace defective products. Smartphone batteries come to mind... Thus, quality can be categorised as hard data, measured via internal data sets that include yield, accidents, rejects, etc.

The other columns on the hard data side of the table refer to volume, cost and time. Volume is generally understood as sales, what the individuals or the overall company does, interim facets of production, etc. Cost could be labour, raw materials, production, overheads and other expenses. Another type of hard data are time, which refers to how long it takes to do something, how long it takes to process a claim, to answer a phone call at a call centre, to design a new product until it hits the market, to produce a widget, to fry a potato chip.

Hard data are measurable, accessible and available. Analysing combinations of these variables (for instance, the relationship between quality and cost, or between quality, time and cost) can lead to different answers, depending on what the analyst is trying to do.

Soft data are a little bit harder to manage. For one thing, soft data are harder to categorise as, by their nature, they are often behavioural, thus less observable and they are also harder to measure and store. For instance, think about punctuality. It should be straightforward to measure: If an employee arrives after the stipulated time, they are considered late. The further they arrive from the stipulated time, the more late they are. This can be measured, as it often is, via a gantry with a personalised entry card that keeps a record of who came in at what time each time a person passes the gantry (the newest technology for this purpose involves face recognition software). However, a challenge in measuring tardiness is how to turn these soft data into some hardish data, as hard as you can make it. An example can be measuring 'excessive breaks'. Most manufacturing companies have breaks. This partic-ular company decided to designate only one place in the parking lot to be the smoking corner for the entire plant. All of a sudden, the company had a problem with excessive work breaks! Supervisors were getting upset because the productivity of their area went down, and they were only going to hire people that did not smoke. The union said that was discrimination, and the affected employees were indignant that they were being penalised. HR analytics helped to uncover the problem: If an employee happened to be working at the other extreme of the plant, it would take them 10 minutes to walk there, 5 minutes to smoke their cigarette and another 10 minutes to walk back. In the end, the company decided to open more spaces to smoke.

Customer service is another type of soft data that gets a lot of attention and is also one that is difficult to turn into hard data because companies tend to receive complaints only from people mostly when they are very upset. Customer satisfaction data can be distorted, especially as they cannot be assumed that if there were no complaints received, it means customers are satisfied. Instead, it could be that the people that complain, if they're still unhappy, they will not necessarily complain again. They will just give up. How to measure this is a challenge!

The point is that some of the soft data are difficult to handle because they are not as straightforward to understand and interpret as hard data. How, then, to turn soft data into credible data? If the marketing department is keeping track of customer complaints, what degree of certainty does the CEO have that this is the full universe of complaints? Companies still continue to struggle with this one, although they have made progress. Amazon, for instance, now sends personalised emails from the person who sold you the item. This makes people more inclined to give a rating. They have also made the scores more credible. This is how they are turning soft data to hard-er data. It takes a bit of time and effort.

Same arguments apply to other soft data, such as loyalty and lost customers. That the company lost the customer – that is relatively easy to find out. Why the customer was lost – that is usually more difficult to determine. It is the same reason that exit interviews are seldom accurate. During an exit interview, employees that are leaving usually do not want to say how much they hate the company; they do not want to burn any bridges.

Work satisfaction is typically measured via annual, or pulse, engagement survey scores. Another way to measure it could be, for instance, by observing changes in the EAP (Employee Assistance Program) patterns. EAP is a benefit that companies have, usually a hotline, where employees can call in when they are experiencing stress. Historically, EAP programs get higher usage during Christmas time, likely because employees get stressed due to emotional issues, not work related. But if this pattern starts to go up in June or September, it is likely that something has happened. Thinking analytically helps to find alternative data, and put it into a model to find out if our hypotheses are supported or not. In this case, we can build a hypothesis that a change in the pattern in the EAP is correlated to turnover, and that it is a lag effect (that is, the impact will only be seen some time later). We can then test for it to see if it is true or not.

There are different ways to determine what data are needed to prove your point. Soft data are quite susceptible to alternative means to achieve that. For example, a company wanted to measure the likelihood of turnover given an employee's last promotion. It were data that previously existed in the HRIS system, but had not been looked at. In looking at these data, a debate ensued on whether the company would end up promoting people who were not ready for the higher-level role. This in turn led to an analysis of the readiness of people who were being hired as compared to the ones that could have been promoted, including the difference in salaries and other associated recruiting costs, and whether or not this cost difference was justified. Analytics allows us to better understand if the company was spending the money wisely in their 'build vs buy' talent dilemma.

Fig. 4.3 shows examples of hard and soft data we can use in answering business questions using HR analytics. To reiterate, in HR we deal with small data – come in hard and soft; most of the hard data would come from various systems like marketing, operations, sales and finance, and most of the soft data come from HR (from internal HRIS system and elsewhere). As the data we need reside in a variety of systems and places across the organisation, and ideally we would like to have them all in one place for ease of access and analysis, we need to build a data warehouse to bring all those data into a single place.

Let's continue the discussion on linking HR variables to business measures. The key concept we emphasise throughout the whole book is that, although you can use HR analytics to address HR issues, this only looks at how HR manages HR; it does not look at how HR helps the business. To make this linkage easier to see, Fig. 4.4 illustrates how different metrics will give you different insights, depending on your need (Forman, 2007).

	Types of Metrics			
	Cost	Time	Volume	Quality
Hire	Recruitment cost ratio	Time to fill	Total number of requisition	Quick quite rate
Reward	Average salary	Time to median compa-ratio	% of employees outside of range	Average compa-ratio of high performers
Manage	Revenue per employee	Time to productivity	Succession pipeline for senior roles	Manager effectiveness
Develop	Training cost as a % of total compensation	Promotion velocity rate	Promotion to external hire ratio	% of roles with >3 successor
Exit	Cost of turnover	Time to fill vacancy	Number of voluntary attrition	% of high performers attrition

Fig. 4.4. Different Metrics Yield Different Insights.

It will be worth it to spend some time digesting this table. For instance, let's look at cost of hire: we can make an assumption that by reducing the cost of hire, we reduce cost to the business by a little but do not necessarily improve overall productivity of the company. This is tactical and only involves how HR does HR. To become more strategic, we need to combine business data with HR data, and start looking for HR reasons why business things change. For example, we can examine, in a manufacturing environment, how years of on-the-job experience are related to product defects. Then, if we find they are negatively correlated (the more experience people have, the lower the product defects), we can also aim to understand if the probability of people staying on the job longer is also linked to the school we hire them from, or to hiring people with prior experience or if we train them the right way for the first six months. In this way, we can use HR analytics to inform the design and development of HR policies/programs/practices that can measurably improve the business.

This approach really works well when we link business variables with HR variables. Ideally, the Y-variable is always a business variable, and the X-variables are a combination of HR variables and business variables. Conversely, if the Y-variable is an HR variable, that will be only of interest to HR and the business is less likely to take notice. If the objective is to reduce turnover, the business still needs to see the connection between turnover and revenue and/or profits. By making the Y-variable a business variable, the model will be answering a question that the business cares about, and that they want answers for. This is the best way to ensure that they will listen.

The likely next question the business will have is, what is the potential payoff or ROI? If the Y-variable is a business variable, then the analysis will be trying to increase revenue or profit. One way to think about ROI is to frame the analysis as profit improvement because we are increasing the top line, or profit improvement because we are reducing the cost line (usually an HR analytics model does not address both at once, as the Y-variable is a single variable). In other words, the aim is to define ROI so that, if the outcome of whatever it is that was uncovered minus what it will cost to make it happen plus the cost of the analysis to get to these data is positive, then the business will benefit from implementing the recommendations. The result can be a percentage of the investment or an absolute amount. If the recommendation can improve profit or reduce cost, minus the cost that it took to get to the answer – like hire a marketing research firm to carry out a study to get the data needed, or implement a new program to resolve the issue at hand, etc. – the benefit minus the cost needs to be positive. If the Y-variable is of the hard data type, it should be relatively straightforward to come up with hypotheses. The business case can then take the form of: 'we're trying to solve a business problem, the success of the business problem we are solving is going to be measured in actual business dollars and it will have a positive ROI.' In this way there is a higher likelihood to get the resources needed to carry out the analysis.

$$ROI = \frac{\text{Project Payoff} - \text{Project Cost}}{\text{Project Cost}}$$

A project's payoff comes in the form of either profit increases or cost savings (through cost reduction or cost avoidance). Some examples are shown below:

Profit Increases:

- Improve sales

- Increase market share

- Introduce new products

- Open new markets

- Enhance customer service

- Increase customer loyalty

Cost Reduction:

- Improve quality

- Reduce cycle time

- Lower downtime

- Decrease complaints

- Prevent employee turnover

- Minimise delays

This short discussion gives an idea of what can be done with HR analytics to improve the impact of HR on the business. To summarise in a practical way, the first thing is to come up with an interesting hypothesis to answer a question that the business is trying to solve. This will gain the trust of management. Next is to determine where the data are and how to manage them. From that point on, it is all about running the model, coming up with insights that inform the hypotheses and to present it to management. Let us take a practical example: An employee in the recruiting area has an idea to figure out channel effectiveness. They want to know if it is better to recruit from one of the job portals, directly from LinkedIn, through referrals, through visits to education institutions or through the company's webpage. Available data indicate that people recruited in the last three years came from one of these different channels. To make it a business problem, you want to investigate if people hired from various channels differ in their time to productivity and in their turnover tendency. These employees can be tracked by source channel – are they still with the company, have they performed well, have they been promoted, what was the turnover rate? The analysis can focus on performance rating, the probability that somebody hired from a specific channel is still in the company and the cost and the time to hire per channel. Maybe the cost and time to hire is lowest with referrals but the quality is not so high. Maybe the most expensive cost is through LinkedIn or job portal because you have to pay fees but the hires are still with the company three years later. An ROI per channel can be estimated in this fashion. The result of this analysis can be a series of recommendations about which channels to emphasise, and which to discontinue, even which educational institutions, based on the insights gained.

Other problems may prove to be less straightforward. Let us say this time that the rewards area has been asked to reduce benefits costs by cutting some employee benefits. The head of the rewards team is not convinced this is a good idea because they suspect that lowering benefits will drive turnover up. From prior analyses, they know that increased turnover is negatively correlated to labour productivity. Thus, they want to delve into the relationship between retention and benefits, even though they know that there are other things at play in retention other than benefits. They will need data from their insurance broker (or from Finance) about the cost of benefits. They also need data on the perceived quality of benefits (maybe an index about how employees value different parts of their benefits package), and data on turnover. Armed with these, the rewards team develop an analysis between potential changes to the benefits package and potential increase in likelihood of turnover. At the end of the analysis, the team concludes that the correlation between benefits and turnover rate is 0.14. One way to look at this result is that there is a very weak correlation, and they should go ahead and start cutting employee benefits. But another way to look at it is that there is some correlation, and that benefits have some role to play in retention, although not a big one. As a next step, the team hypothesises that there is a combination of elements that, together, drive turnover. Then you run the model twice: once with benefits in it, and one without benefits in it. This will show how much worse the predictability of the model is when benefits are taken out. If the complete model has a correlation of 0.75, and without benefits it drops to 0.4, it is reasonable to say that benefits are worth keeping.

The following is an illustrative list of potential analytics projects across the HR value chain:

Recruitment:

- Determine the combination of values, competencies and skills for best fit and performance.

- Develop different combinations for different job families and hierarchical levels.

- Ascertain which sources of candidates yield the best cost-benefit.

- Analyse labour market skill availability vs. internal needs.

Learning and Development:

- Determine optimal onboarding patterns to reduce quick exits.

- Evaluate application of learning by different demographics.

- Create career paths and suitable development strategies.

Remuneration:

- Calculate ROI of various pay schemes.

- Estimate cost vs. Perceived value curves.

- Identify patterns of compensation vs. performance to forecast turnover rates.

Career Management:

- What behaviours, skills and attributes best fit the current and future leadership needs of the organisation.

- Identify High Potentials via combinations of competencies, skills, values and performance.

- Determine potential promotions via network analysis.

4.2 DATA ANALYSIS QUESTION TYPES

There are several types of data analysis questions; we list the main ones as follows:

A **descriptive** question is one that seeks to summarise a characteristic of a set of data.

An **exploratory** question is one in which you analyse the data to see if there are patterns, trends or relationships between variables. These types of analyses are also called 'hypothesis-generating' analyses because, rather than testing a hypothesis as would be done with an inferential, causal or mechanistic question, you are looking for patterns that would support proposing a hypothesis.

An **inferential** question is a restatement of this proposed hypothesis as a question and would be answered by analysing a different set of data.

A **predictive** question is where you ask which groups of people will resign during the next year. In this type of question you are less interested in what causes someone to resign, just in predicting whether someone will actually resign.

A **causal** question asks about whether changing one factor will change another factor, on average, in a population.

For more information on these concepts, see the article 'What is the question?' by Leek & Peng, on Science, Vol. 347, Issue 6228, March 2015 (https://science.sciencemag.org/content/347/6228/1314/F1).

4.3 BUILDING MODELS

Building hypotheses is important for 'testing' the causes of business issues:

- Hypotheses **are the bridge** between the business questions and the data gathering.

- Devising a good hypothesis also aids in **determining the right analytical approach.**

- Starting with a hypothesis helps to ensure that the analysis and conclusions **will not be biased** by pre-conceived notions.

There are a number of good practices when developing a hypothesis. We do not need to get too technical for our purposes – researchers and academics follow a stricter protocol than the one we describe here – and yet, we cannot overemphasise the importance of starting each HR analytics project with a solid set of hypotheses.

To begin with, write a hypothesis as a statement, not as a question. Hypotheses are informed, testable explanations or predictions.

Use relevant literature to inform the hypothesis. Organisational psychology and management scholars have accumulated a wealth of knowledge on the causes and consequences of various problems.

When a draft is ready, discuss the hypothesis with the project sponsor. Ensure it accurately reflects the business situation being looked at.

Ensure clarity. A good hypothesis is written in clear and simple language. Reading the hypothesis should clarify whether each possible analysis result will support or reject the hypothesis.

Make sure the hypothesis is testable. A single refutation of a hypothesis shifts the attention to a different line of thinking. Proceed when hypotheses are not rejected.

4.3.1 Testing Hypotheses

- **Null hypothesis (H0)** is the hypothesis that is directly tested – usually a statement that the parameter value has no effect. To follow our prior example on recruiting channels, a H0 would say that there are no differences in performance attributed to the source channel. That is, it does not matter where people are hired from, the results are the same. This may seem an odd way to phrase a hypothesis, when what wanting to prove is the exact opposite; but remember that we want to *reject* this hypothesis!

- **Alternative hypothesis (H1)** is a hypothesis that contradicts the H0. This hypothesis states that the parameter falls in some alternative set of values to what the H0 specifies.

- The **p-value is the probability**, if H0 were true, that the test statistic would fall in this collection of values.

To be valid, all significance tests require certain assumptions. These assumptions refer to the type of data, the form of the population distribution, the method of sampling and the sample size. A significance test is conducted to determine if the data contradict the H0.

The H1 is supported if the H0 appears to be incorrect.

4.3.2 Blueprint for Analytics

Let us break down an example of how these concepts can be applied in an actual situation.

1. **Frame business question:** For instance, we are losing customers due to poor after-sales service.

2. **Develop hypotheses** (What may be causing the problem?): High turnover in the after-sales department due to:

   - Our total compensation is uncompetitive

   - Pay for performance differentiation is inadequate

   - Lack of leadership skills in the after-sales area

   - Insufficient training

3. **How can we prove/disprove?** Identify evidence for the hypotheses

   - Customer complaints are related to not being able to find the people they had earlier spoken to and are frustrated that their issues, which they had already highlighted to the service rep, are still unresolved

   - Internal analysis confirms that, in the majority of the cases, complaints are coming from customers that were assigned to service reps that have since left the company

   - Most people that left in the last six months were paid below target pay

   - When we are losing high performers that are paid at the top end of the range, it may be a sign that our upside is inadequate (note that this is a new hypothesis derived from the insights gained in the analysis)

   - However, all other hypotheses were not supported in this case (that is, performance differentiation works, no differences due to training, leadership competencies are similar to that in other areas of the business)

4. What analyses should we run? Analyses needed to support the evidence:

   • Incumbent-based analysis to measure if there is any correlation between pay and attrition

   • Percentage of top performers that resigned

5. What data are required? List of data required to run the analysis

6. Responsibility and timeline. Define roles, responsibilities and expected completion dates

7. Plot the projects according to the expected impact and amount of complexity involved as per Fig. 4.5.

There is a useful model (Evaluation Planning & The 'V' Model, by ROI Institute Canada https://roiinstitutecanada.com/roi-methodology/evaluation-planning-the-v-model/) which can help in achieving business alignment.

On the left side of this 'V' model are listed the different needs the business may have that relate to the analysis being proposed. On the right side are the ways to evaluate if these needs are being met. The middle column shows the objectives for each level of need being addressed:

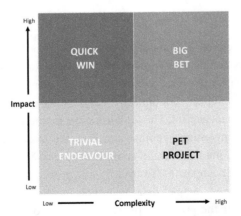

Fig. 4.5. Expected Impact and Amount of Complexity of Projects.

Level 1: Preferences for the program are defined (implementation)

Level 2: The information, knowledge or skills that are required to address the performance needs are identified.

Level 3: Performance that must change or action that must be taken to address the business needs (hypotheses).

Level 4: Specific business measures that need improvement to take advantage of the payoff opportunity (problem statement).

Level 5: Possibility for a ROI before the solution is pursued.

It is worth noting that this model building is iterative. Ultimately a model's usefulness depends on how closely the data mirror the real world. A statistical model serves two key purposes in a data analysis, which are to: Provide a quantitative summary of your data (data reduction) and to impose a specific structure on the population from which the data were sampled (how the world works and how the data were generated).

Selecting a model will depend on:

- The problem as defined

- The relevance and availability of data

- The time period to be forecast

- The patterns (trend, seasonal, cyclical or irregular) that exist in the data

There is a danger in jumping to conclusions about the problem without first testing a series of hypotheses. Take, for instance, a case where high attrition is viewed from an employee life cycle perspective, coupled with 'intuitive' expectations of outcomes from the part of management. The seeds are sown to catalyse the forming of various interesting hypotheses around the mismatch of hiring expectations, misalignment of compensation and non-transparency of career development. Instead, with proper formulation of hypotheses and simple data collection techniques, one could conclude that the problem arises rather from poor design of the performance appraisal process, for example. This can then be tested, along with the interdependence of employee skills and competencies with organisational culture, as lock-and-key mechanisms for employee success.

4.4 SUPERVISED AND UNSUPERVISED METHODS

4.4.1 Defining Supervised vs Unsupervised Methods

When we talk about **unsupervised** methods, we mean that there is no specific purpose or target being specified; for example, 'Do our employees or customers naturally fall into different groups?'

Supervised, on the other hand, means that there is a specific purpose or target being defined; for example, 'Can we find groups of employees or customers who have a particularly high likelihood of doing X?'

4.4.2 Common Types of Algorithms

There are a variety of common algorithms to ease in the selection of an analytical approach. The main ones are as follows:

Classification: Attempt to predict each individual in a population to obtain the probability of which class they belong to ('How likely will "x" happen?') – Supervised

Regression: Attempts to predict the numerical value of some variable for that individual ('How much will "x" happen?') – Supervised

Similarity Matching: Attempts to identify similar individuals based on data known about them – Supervised/Unsupervised

Clustering: Attempts to group individuals in a population together by their similarity (Not driven by any specific purpose) – Unsupervised

Different algorithms can be of use in different circumstances, which is why it is useful to know these.

4.4.3 Evaluating Model Performance

To determine the usefulness of any model, it is necessary to consider the implications of the results obtained, which can serve as a guide in determining what actions to take. The key things to look for are as follows:

Directionality: The directionality of the relationship is positive, meaning that as X increases, Y increases, or negative, meaning that as X increases, Y decreases (or vice versa).

Magnitude: The number of units that Y increases (or decreases) by per additional 1 unit of X. What is important is to determine if this change in Y for each change of one unit in X is meaningful based on the context.

Uncertainty: In statistical terms, results are often stated as probabilities. It is common to see results in terms of a confidence interval, which is a range of values that also contains the true result for the population (e.g. 'the answer is somewhere between this and that number').

Coefficient of Determination (r^2): This is often the measure of the strength of a model and is defined as the proportion of the variance in the dependent variable that is predictable from the independent variable(s)

Root Mean Square Error (RMSE): Measures the difference between the values predicted by the model and the actual values observed. It is interpreted as the standard deviation of the unexplained variance.

In the above-mentioned example (see Fig. 4.6), the model is a straight line, with a positive direction, a magnitude of 0.7919 and an r^2 of 0.692.

Two other useful concepts to evaluate a model are Sensitivity and Specifity:

- **Sensitivity** of the model: % of correctly predicted 'Yes' (True Positive Rate)

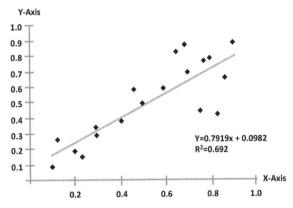

Fig. 4.6. Illustration of a Straight Line Model.

	Condition: Positive	Condition: Negative
Predicted: Positive	True Positive	False Positive (Type I)
Predicted: Negative	False Negative (Type II)	True Negative
	Sensitivity = True Positive Rate	Specificity = True Negative Rate

Fig. 4.7. Sensitivity and Specificity.

- **Specificity** of the model: % of correctly predicted 'No' (True Negative Rate)

Fig. 4.7 illustrates these concepts.

SUMMARY

In this chapter, we have covered:

- The details of the analytics design framework
- Data analysis question types and flow chart

- Model building overview

- Supervised and unsupervised methods

QUESTIONS

TELCO-A recently rolled out a new offer –
Internet bundle, i-FAST

During a meeting with top management, the executives
posted a question to the team:

'Among our existing customers, who
are likely to respond to this new
product?'

As part of the team, which data mining algorithm will
you use for analysis?

In 2013, B-Corp. introduced a new online
learning system.

The senior leaders are now considering to shut down the
learning platform. Prior to making any decisions, they
sought HR's opinions:

'How much will our employees use the
system moving forward? If the
predicted usage is high, the system will
not be removed'

As a HR Manager, what data mining algorithm will you
use to help make the decision?

Examples: Insights through Analytics

Determining Impact Quantitatively Through Workforce Maps

ATTRACTION	**DEVELOPMENT**	**RETENTION**
Who comes into the organisation?	How do people move through the organisation, through different assignments, jobs and levels of responsibility?	Who is staying and who is leaving?
How successful is the organisation at drawing in the kinds of people it needs to achieve its goals?	How successful is the organisation at growing and nurturing the talent it needs to execute its business strategy?	How successful is the organisation at retaining people who have the right capabilities and produce the highest value?

Interpreting a Workforce Map

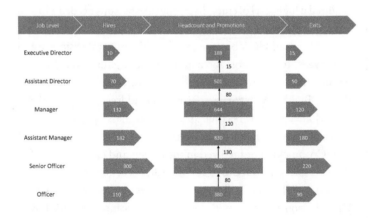

Would you conclude, based on the chart shown, that the company has a high attrition problem? Why or why not? Should this be a concern to the business? What hypothesis or hypotheses can you come up with to explain these results? How would you test your hypotheses?

A Global Bank[1]

This international bank is well known for its talent practices. However, it was not too long ago that it had no data warehouse – no data to justify ROI for HR practices.

When the bank first started their Human Capital Analytics (HCA) program, the bank was undergoing a temporary business adjustment due to regulatory restrictions. A primary motivation to start HCA was that the bank did not want to significantly reduce their headcount in the interim. Instead, they wanted to explore talent redeployment as the first option.

The bank had a look internally and realised it was sitting on a pile of information about the staff. The first task was to start with psychometric profiling of employees: can the salesperson do what the debt collectors currently do; and can the debt collectors do what the salesperson does. The skills seemed similar on the surface. However, the initial finding showed that debt collectors required a high level of empathy, while salespersons needed a low level of empathy. That was how HCA got started at the bank.

The focus of HCA became to help make better decisions for employees, for the workforce and for the organisation. More importantly, it is about connecting HR to business outcomes (Pease, Byerly, & Fitz-enz, 2013). This addressed one of the HR challenges to become trusted business partners, by wanting to own the business outcome.

HCA quickly got involved in the design and calculations of the variable sales incentive for the sales workforce in all the branches. When HCA first started this role, they approached HR: 'do you want to own this, as this is compensation'. HR said, 'not really, I think this is a business problem. You can decide how to pay as long as you stay within budget.' Nevertheless, HCA was able to bring to the fore findings regarding what worked and what didn't in terms of sales incentives, whereby cost and ROI can be the same but the

---

[1] With thanks to Eric Sandosham for his invaluable contribution to this section.

sales results can be very different. These positive results led HR to embrace these analytics to shape these decisions around employees that lead to a business outcome.

In the hiring space what has emerged from the HCA research is that university grades do not matter much when it comes to predicting future performance. It is important to pass and get the certificate, but in reality, having 'A' grades does not matter. The recruiting area has reduced the weight given to grades. There is now a minimum bar for grades, but anything above that bar is ok. That bar is not an 'A', it's a B or B+ grade. In fact, HCA found that there is an inverted-U correlation between grades and the ability to solve problems. Generally, if grades were very low, it may be due to a lack of technical skills. If another candidate had better grades, the likelihood is they will be better performers. So the curve went up. But somewhere near the middle of the grade range, the curve started to come down with every increase in GPA. It was not even a flattening of the curve; it came down. At the time the HCA team reasoned with the recruiting team that candidates with very high GPA spent less time at school developing life or social skills. So, when they are placed in a work setting, they have difficulty interacting with others. This makes them less ideal to settle into a fast-paced, highly interdependent culture at the bank.

Another area HCA found worth solving was in the training space; they observed that there is a large amount of training that goes on, but no one knew what was the ROI. The organisation was struggling with that because training programs are about accessibility and trying to make training available to all employees. Thus, nobody in HR wants to say: 'I don't think you should go for this training as you won't get any value out of it.' Training ROI became increasingly important in defining if the organisation was to invest in training for one individual but not for others, or if one type of training made more sense than another.

HCA also found performance appraisals to be very highly biased. There were issues with the collective understanding of the meaning of 'fair', 'good', 'better' performance. There was also the issue of halo effects: 'I like one individual better than the other', and of recency effects whereby an employee can do a good job the whole year, but in the last month of the year they took it easy and the boss only remembers that. It does not necessarily nullify the appraisal but, ultimately, it affects it. The recency effect also applies to someone doing mediocre for the year and the last month they did fantastically well. The idea was that performance appraisals had several issues diminishing its usefulness, and HCA went to work to uncover these issues.

Another problem HCA was looking at was promotions: Managers were more likely to promote people like themselves. For example, if a successful boss needs a replacement, then he/she will find someone with similar competencies to do this job. Very rarely are managers saying: 'I'm promoting someone who will be needed in the next five years because the environment is going to change; we don't need someone like me'. HCA wants to look into promotions with a view to future-proof the organisation. In other words, taking what the organisation knows about how the future will be like and incorporating this information into the assessment of future leaders.

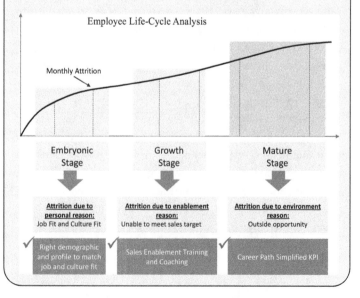

PART II: APPLICATIONS

5

TURNOVER

5.1 SIMPLE HR ANALYTICS ARE USEFUL TOO

An undercurrent to this book, different from most writing on this topic, is that HR analytics is accessible to all in the HR department, as long as each HR practitioner remembers the need for data to speak for them when making their case to management, or to employees. With little much else than Excel, some data, knowledge of basic statistics and analytical thinking, all HR professionals can have significant impact in how a company carries our HR and adds value. In fact, the example we will detail below showcases that it is actually possible to model a problem more by intuition and coincidence than by design, and still arrive at a workable set of recommendations that will help the company improve. Even a flawed analysis in more ways than one, as the one we will describe, can be useful and become part of how HR is being done in the company. It is this belief: that anyone can learn and apply simple yet powerful HR analytics, that drove us to write this book.

In the example below, the HR team certainly didn't set out to change HR's approach to dealing with problems. At that time, they only wanted to showcase the point that turnover was not caused by HR, or at least not by HR alone, as the line management were portraying it. But one thing was true – what they were trying to do is to make the company better, by putting as much rigour as best we could behind HR decisions. As limited as their resources were at that time, as short-sighted as their approach was at that time, they still had much impact on the company. Imagine what you, the reader, will be able to do with far more knowledge about how to approach HR problems with data, and with far better tools to do so. The point of this chapter is that, even in a limited tool/data/ knowledge scenario, it is still possible to have a big impact, by following the principles of developing the hypotheses, testing them and letting the data talk, looking at every graph and seeing what story the graphs tell and then pursue it, and to have the patience to go after it. Some of the analyses will pay out, some will not. Of every hypothesis tested, some will give fruits, some will not; that is ok. Even the ones that do not help to determine that the path was not the right one and allow for correcting the course.

The first example is a flawed one, but a good one, because it had success. Flawed because it did not follow an analytical method, it did not have absolutely clean data and did not have clear hypotheses when the project started. The team was really just trying to figure this out without a map. The second example, in contrast, shows how turnover can be tackled with more powerful analytics.

5.2 CASE OF A SEMICONDUCTOR COMPANY IN INDIA

The way semiconductor companies earn revenue starts with bidding for – and winning – projects for clients. For instance, if Apple wants a chip for their upcoming Apple 'XX', whichever Original Equipment Manufacturer (OEM) is doing the design for Apple would ask the semiconductor companies to bid. The OEM would usually give the specifications and the budget, say it should have all these cool new features and cost less than $50 per chip. The different semiconductor companies would then design a chip that matches the specifications and cost given, and Apple would then choose which company they want to work with. Usually, the bids have a strict deadline; the companies must submit the design bid to the OEM by a certain date and time – this is called 'closing of the project' in the semiconductor business.

The company had missed on a string of highly lucrative projects in the electronics industry, and was struggling to find revenue sources. The cause, according to management, of missing deadlines repeatedly at that time was due to high turnover in the design teams, mostly in India.

From a business point of view, being able to complete projects by the deadline was a crucial part of the strategy. And the staff turnover in India was high at that time: rates were in the high 20s, (which means that nearly 3 people out of every 10 employees left the company in that year) mostly at entry levels and the next two levels up. The HR team was asked to figure out how to lower turnover, not because turnover in itself was the problem, but because the company was not able to meet the design deadlines and close projects on time.

Initially, the HR team in India tackled this problem in the traditional way, that is to say, management said pay was the problem – which was the fault of HR – and that's the place to start. To date, the company pegged salaries to the market, following competitors in terms of salary levels, pay increases and retention schemes, and was satisfied to see that turnover rates were in line with other local companies in the industry. Management's challenge was that keeping up with local market trends was not enough; the company needed to be below others in turnover, or better still, above the rest in labour productivity. The HR team aimed to achieve this objective.

5.2.1 Design

From the beginning, the HR team knew that a level of zero turnover was not only unattainable, but perhaps unhealthy. The company has in place a forced-curve performance management philosophy, and wanted turnover to be roughly in line with the expected percentage of lowest performers. Thus, the team embarked on a quest to not only reduce turnover by 25%, but also to reduce turnover at the highest levels of performance to as close to zero as possible.

As a starting point, the HR team analysed the HR practices around recruiting, pay and development, which they thought could potentially have an impact on turnover rates. They also carried out an in-depth analysis of turnover and retention at the India Design Centres. In doing so, we followed these principles:

- **Support the business** – The HR team was keen to help the business reduce turnover so that projects could be closed on time.

- **Reduce turnover** – It was critical to understand what was driving unwanted turnover in the organisation. From day one, the team went beyond the pay-related hypothesis and looked for other causes of turnover they could impact.

- **Evidence-driven** – One of the beliefs held by management team was that turnover among female employees was higher. Another example was the debate on whether new hires from top educational institutions were better. The HR team sought to end these 'my-opinions-are-better-than-yours' discussions by bringing in unequivocal data.

- **Measurable impact** – The end result had to be business improvement in the form of more projects closed on time. Not simply an improvement in turnover rate or an increase in Employee Opinion Survey results.

5.2.2 Hypotheses/Drivers

The team started asking themselves logical questions, like: If it's not pay, then what is it? And how can we prove it? This desire to prove themselves right, that turnover was not HR's fault, is what drove this piece of the work. The team then wanted to understand the reasons for turnover. They developed a comprehensive list of drivers of turnover through interviews with managers, employees and HR staff, including the results of the exit interviews of the last two to three years.

The first issue the team addressed was that the answers to the interviews from management and the other groups were inconsistent with the results of the exit interviews. When looking at them closely, the reasons given usually were clustered around 'leaving for personal reasons', or 'pursuing another better opportunity', which the team thought lacked credibility. To counter this, the team opted to do a fresh set of interviews – through a market research firm – with employees that had resigned from the company in the prior three years. They managed to interview 77% of over 240 former employees. In the interview, they were asked again the reasons why they left the company. This approach yielded much better results than the original exit interviews. For the employees interviewed, the top three reasons for turnover accounted for 71% of total attrition. These top three reasons were (See Fig. 5.1) as follows:

- Pursue Higher Studies: Employees left to pursue a higher degree in their field.

- Relocation: The employees left to live closer to their own or their spouses' hometown.

- Dissatisfaction with job: This item refers to whether the employees thought, or not, that the company was delivering on the promise made to them when they were being recruited.

The team had another idea: they shouldn't only be asking people why they left; what they should be doing is asking the people who were working at the company, why they were still there – why haven't they left? To do this, they ran a few focus groups to find out why people were staying, which was what they were trying to understand!

Armed with data from management, employees that had left, employees that have stayed and other members of the HR team, they categorised the reasons why people left and why they stayed into three categories. The first category consisted of **external reasons**, which included some they expected to find, like: 'I went to study my Masters', as well as other reasons that were somewhat different from what was expected like 'the work location is too far from where I live'.

Top Attrition Reasons	Job Levels		
	Level 1	Level 2	Level 3
Higher Studies	30%	15%	10%
Job Profile	25%	24%	30%
Relocation	20%	20%	8%
Better Pay	5%	10%	15%

Fig. 5.1. Top Attrition Reasons.

The second category was **organisational reasons**. Besides pay, which they knew they had to address, they found a few interesting things, like: 'I haven't been promoted since I joined', or 'I believed the marketing pitch that, with six different divisions, this company would allow me to move from one division to the next, but that didn't happen' and 'It turns out that everybody above me only has ever worked in one division, so I don't want to work in only one area'. The team suspected that what prospects were being offered while being recruited was not panning out once they joined.

The third category was **individual reasons**. For many of the women interviewed, the reason was: 'I'm going to get married' – remember this is in India, where many marriages are arranged. A typical story from these former female employees is that, after graduating, they work for one or two to three years, until the future mother-in-law shows up saying: 'time to get married'. Getting married, to them, meant giving up the work and moving back to where the mother-in-law lives, having babies and helping around the house. This finding appeared to support management's view that females have a higher turnover rate.

This first level of fact-finding yielded three categories of drivers, as shown below:

- External Drivers:
  - Pay Levels
  - Competition
  - Overseas Opportunities

- Organizational Drivers:
  - Job Profiles
  - Involuntary Resignations
  - Performance Ratings
  - Dissatisfaction with Manager
  - Promotion Opportunities

- Individual Drivers:
  - Higher Education
  - Relocation
  - Low Performance
  - Educational Institution
  - Tenure
  - Gender

These became the hypotheses in a sense: that each of these variables had a role to play in turnover, and that pay alone was not the cause. The next step was to find out which of these were the more crucial ones.

5.2.3 Data Gathering and Analysis

5.2.3.1. External drivers

5.2.3.1.1. Pay levels. The first review was the impact of pay on turnover, as this was the original question from management. However, the phone interview data said that less than 10% of employees left for pay reasons. The team then looked at the compa-ratios for these employees at the time they left, and found that in only five cases the compa-ratio was below the company median. This finding led the team to do additional research (see Fig. 5.2). Even though it was clear that pay was not a major cause of turnover, the team became concerned with the number of individuals who had the highest performance rating (rating of 1 out of 5 levels, where level 5 meant that the employee was too new to be appraised) but were paid below 0.9 compa-ratio. This led to the development of a new HR policy to ensure that top rated employees would be paid no less than 10% below their salary grade midpoint.

Looking at this graph, it was apparent that compensation was not aligned with performance. For instance, there are many

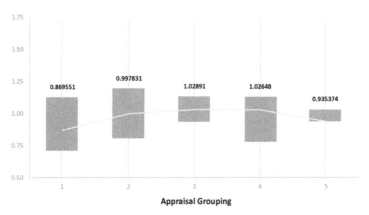

Appraisal Grouping

Fig. 5.2. Compa-ratio vs Performance Rating.

employees with a 3 or 4 rating who were highly paid. As a result, the team recommended the redesign of the merit increase tables, to better align compa-ratio and performance levels. However, the team also compared pay against years of experience by salary grade, and found no significant differences. Nor were there any insights from the analyses of the other external drivers.

5.2.3.2. Organizational drivers

5.2.3.2.1. Performance ratings. The analysis of turnover by performance level revealed that the company was losing more employees rated 1 and 2 (top performers) than expected. This was cause for concern as this was precisely the employees they wanted most to retain (see Fig. 5.3).

5.2.3.2.2. Dissatisfaction with managers. One of the hypotheses the team looked into was how much did managers affect turnover rates. The team collected data on the turnover rate per manager. What they found, surprised them. Fig. 5.4 shows the managers, the Business Group they belong to, the percentage of turnover, the rating of those employees turning over, the performance rating of the managers themselves and the overall satisfaction index for the manager in the employee survey.

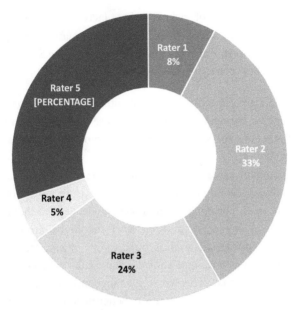

Fig. 5.3. Turnover by Performance Rating.

Business Unit	Manager	Turnover Profile	Turnover %	Manager Performance Rating	Employee Survey Manager Score
BU 1	A	3 (Rater 2, 5), 2 (Rater 3)	67%	2	0.26
BU 2	B	4 (Rater 1, 2), 4 (Rater 3)	62%	1	0.38
BU 3	C	2 (Rater 1, 2), 2 (Rater 3)	50%	2	0.52
BU 3	D	2 (Rater 1, 5), 1 (Rater 3)	50%	1	0.65
BU 4	E	4 (Rater 1, 2, 5), 2 (Rater 3)	47%	1	0.06
BU 1	F	5 (Rater2, 5)	42%	1	0.23
BU 5	G	4 (Rater 2, 5)	40%	2	0.15
BU 3	H	3 (Rater 1,2)	38%	2	0.58
BU 4	I	3 (Rater 2), 2 (Rater 3)	36%	2	0.29
BU 3	J	2 (Rater5), 1 (Rater 3)	33%	1	0.51
BU 6	K	2 (Rater 2, 5)	33%	2	0.52
BU 7	L	5 (Rater 2, 5)	31%	2	0.73
BU 7	M	4 (Rater 2, 5)	31%	2	0.61
BU 7	N	4 (Rater 2, 5), 1 (Rater 3)	28%	2	0.44
BU 3	O	1 (Rater 2), 2 (Rater 3, 4)	27%	2	0.28
BU 6	P	2 (Rater 2, 5)	27%	2	0.43
BU 1	Q	5 (Rater 2, 5)	27%	1	0.18

Fig. 5.4. Managers with Highest Attrition.

The table shows that the top 15 highest attrition managers lost more employees rated 1 and vs employees rated 3 or 4. The surprising finding was that many of these managers received a rating of 1 by their superiors. This led to several discussions with senior management (the ones giving the top ratings to these managers) about the importance of including these facts in their appraisal of their direct reports, and a change to the performance management criteria so that turnover rates (but not the Employee Survey score) would be a key metric for all managers.

5.2.3.2.3. Promotion opportunities.

Another result was that a high percentage of the employees that left were high performers with several years of experience. These were employees who were ready for a promotion.

The company career planning guidelines established the number of years that it should take an average employee to move from one level to the next. The implication of these guidelines was that no less than 15% of employees at each level should be promoted to maintain an appropriate level of 'build vs buy' talent. The analysis of promotion opportunities showed that actual promotion rates were lower than that. This led to a change in promotion criteria, training and job rotation programs to better tie-in with the intended developmental outcomes.

An analysis of the market pay differentials between the three levels of employees under study showed that these were in the range of 50–75%. The average market salary increase in our industry for the prior year was around 15%. The company used this number to budget increases and to adjust salary range midpoints. Obviously, if the midpoints move the same as the average increase, employees generally will have difficulty to move up the salary range. The implications were that, because the company was not promoting employees fast enough, they left. This meant hiring from the market to cover the vacancies. However, these newly hired employees from the outside were paid at a premium above the market rate. The resulting differential in salary levels between the employees that had stayed and those coming in, created additional problems ('the best way to get a salary increase in this company is to leave and come back'). These findings, combined, led to changes in the recruitment compensation policies.

5.2.3.3. Individual drivers

5.2.3.3.1. Educational institution.

One of the strongest-held beliefs of managers (and of the HR recruiters as well!) was that new students from Tier 1 educational institutions would become better employees than those from Tier 2 schools. The team took the opportunity to determine if Tier 1 students were more likely to have higher performance ratings and/or stay longer with the company than Tier 2 students. The analysis did not show any difference in performance ratings from Tier 1 to Tier 2, but uncovered that Tier 1 entry-level employees were more inclined to leave sooner and go for higher education, and they were also paid higher, making it a 'bad deal' for the company, as there was no difference in performance, the cost was higher as was the turnover rate. This also led to a change in recruitment sources.

5.2.3.3.2. Tenure. An analysis of turnover against tenure revealed that the highest attrition was among employees between one and two years of tenure with the company (Fig. 5.5). This finding pointed to deficiencies in the recruitment, selection and onboarding processes.

5.2.3.3.3. Gender. Female turnover was slightly higher than male turnover. However, female median tenure was better than that for males. This finding led to changes in the support groups for females, including the implementation of a 'mother-in-law day', aimed at showing these future relatives the importance of the work their

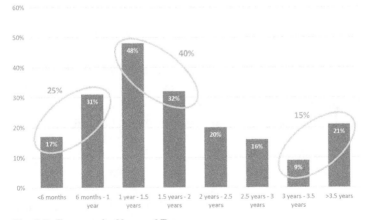

Fig. 5.5. Turnover by Years of Tenure.

future daughters-in-law were doing, and perhaps consider post-poning the wedding for a time.

5.2.4 Insights

The company was clearly suffering from high turnover which affected productivity and revenue generation opportunities. Over-all, the company was losing almost as many employees as they were hiring above entry level and, as a consequence, they were hiring, at a premium, nearly as many employees at the supervisor level as they were losing in the team leader level, also at a premium in pay.

This study aided the HR team in making several changes to policies aimed at increasing retention, and hopefully revenue growth. These included changes to recruiting profiles, manager and employee training programs, career planning and development plans and pay policies. The results were that turnover was reduced by 30%.

However, as successful as this initiative was, both to the company and to employees, the fact is that it required very little by way of statistics, big data warehouses, sophisticated tools and, if we are completely honest here, some of the findings were not part of the original hypotheses, but rather a consequence of prior work that was inconclusive, which led the team to dig deeper. Special note goes to the presentation of insights: especially the table that shows turnover by manager. It is worth remembering that the whole project started on the premise, by management, that turnover was due to HR. This chart made it clear that, at a minimum, it was a shared problem, which opened up the possibility to discuss changes in policies and their implementation that otherwise may not have happened. In this instance, it was not the beauty of the analysis that won the day. Perhaps it was that they had no counter-argument. It is one thing to disagree with people, and quite another to disagree with data.

5.3 CASE OF A BANK IN SINGAPORE

This large Singaporean bank also had a problem with early salesforce attrition: 40% of new recruits leave within the first eight months. The bank, however, felt that they were quite rigorous in their selection process: candidates went through multiple interviews, as well as psychometric testing. The recruiting team captured a variety of data, and they asked the HR analytics team to help them make sense of it to determine the causes of these 'quick exits'.

Initially, the HR analytics team asked questions from the recruiting team, and from management, to understand the processes and, as a result, created a large mind map for the recruiting team. This tool was aimed at framing the collection of data in the following categories: hiring, onboarding and supervision. The map served to develop a set of hypotheses and of questions intended to guide the search for data.

For hiring, questions for data gathering included competencies, past experiences (previous jobs or fresh graduates), results of assessment tests (personality traits), demographics, etc.

Related to their onboarding, questions included goals given, where were the new employees assigned (e.g. in Singapore, different locations provide different sales opportunities, as certain branches inherently have more client traffic). Location was also examined in terms of distance from work to home, including arrival time.

There were also questions about supervision. A few of the questions posed were about team integrity, like are there certain cliques that happen? (One of the observations from line management was that, often, in some of the five-people teams, there was always one new employee leaving but the original four always stayed, so they suspected the four existing members rejected the new ones). The team also asked if employees left the bank when their supervisors moved jobs, especially if they had left the bank as well. Other questions explored interview bias. The HR analytics team wanted to know who did the interviews. Can the attrition be traced back to specific interviewers?

At first, the HR analytics team collected the data and went to work trying to correlate everything, to see what pops out. They thought that they did not know enough about why people would come and leave so quickly in this professionally run bank, and thought that by collecting data widely and looking for correlations, they could find some answers.

And they did; for instance, they found that if people were assigned to locations which were too distant from their home, they had a much higher probability of leaving. They also found that there were interview biases. Some supervisors wanted to only hire a particular type of employee because they believed they were the best type; these supervisors would over-ride the psychometric test results, under the premise that they were experienced salespeople and knew what was best for the bank. But it actually did not work out; it turned out the psychometric score was usually correct and the employees hired by the supervisor over-riding ended up leaving.

But, as the team discussed the data with the recruiting team and the line, new questions came up. For instance, during onboarding, how did the new employees learn about the incentive scheme? The team found that new employees only learn about the incentive scheme when they are placed in the branch. And that some of them go for 1–1.5 months of training about how banking products work, with no one explaining to them how they earn money. For these new employees, the first day they are in the branch, and need to hit the sales target, that's when they learn about the sales incentive. The senior sales management did not know this was happening.

In light of these unexpected findings, the HR analytics team decided to follow a more rigorous HR analytical approach to better frame the problem. The biggest change came in reframing early salesforce attrition as the symptom – not the problem. To frame this as a problem, they asked different, business-focused questions, such as: Is the bank losing revenue opportunities?

Once the problem was framed in business terms, the team went on to trace the process directly in the field as passive observers. This way they could place themselves in the shoes of the people going through the process, be it recruiters, supervisors, new employees or existing employees. The HR analytics team realised that having available data was not enough unless they could contextualise them. By immersing themselves in the process they were able to understand it and thus add meaning and nuance to the data. For instance, they produced a table (See Fig. 5.6) of Job Classification and KPI setting which not only served to standardise this process, but also to highlight that the information contained was complex and that supervisors across the bank branches were not consistent

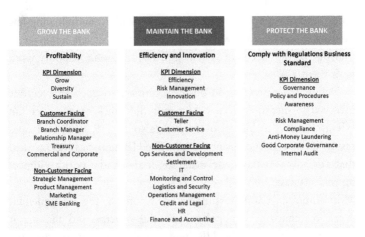

Fig. 5.6. Job Classification and HR Dimensions.

in communicating it. Armed with this new knowledge, they went on to develop the hypothesis: Can quality of hiring be the cause of the quick exits?

The HR analytics team set out to collect data anew. Earlier they had collected data without proper hypotheses, and realised the analyses were incomplete because they did not really know what they were looking for. This time, by being specific in what they were looking for, they were confident they would find it.

The analytical solution yielded impactful results. One of these ended up becoming a hiring policy change; the team found that off-the-shelf psychometric tests did reduce hiring bias but could not be used by themselves in making hiring decisions. These had to be customised for the culture of the company. The current testing could only differentiate for potential best and worst employees, but had no ability to discern in between these two groups. The combination of adjusted testing with standardised supervisor questions (and a guideline for evaluation of answers, especially culture-related answers) provided better information to avoid quick exits.

The analyses also allowed the team to predict certain behaviours and intervene. In particular, they developed a predictive model to highlight when a new employee was not meeting targets and was showing signs of distress, as it was found that this behaviour was highly correlated to the employee leaving within the following few months. The HR team was then able to know which employee to pull out of the incentive system and do additional support work with them.

Defining the problem in business terms also allowed everyone involved to measure success. Not only did quick exits reduce (an HR goal), cost to hire also reduced (also an HR goal) and sales results improved (the business goal). The HR analytics was satisfied that not only was the model accurate, it also had a positive impact on the business.

In addition, it was possible to operationalise the recommendations, by changing the policy and the process and making it recurring. This way, the HR analytics can step away, and the process will continue to run indefinitely.

SUMMARY

A few conclusions from these two cases:

1. Solve for business problems, not HR symptoms.

2. Go for causation, rather than exploit the correlation. HR analytics is different than, say, marketing analytics. In marketing analytics, the aim is to sell the next best offer to a customer. In this case, if certain behaviours have very strong indications that you need a product, correlation is sufficient enough to gain value from the information. In HR, to understand why the employee is manifesting himself/herself to go on leave, and is at risk of attrition, it is important to also understand why he/she is feeling that why – is it a supervisor problem, or competition problem.

3. HR data can be highly biased. Frequently stakeholders think they already 'know' the answer, so why bother? In these cases, it is best to go in with an open mind, and to collect new pieces of data to counter the potential bias. Fig. 5.7 illustrates how data can show that the managers' 'gut' was not as good as they thought.

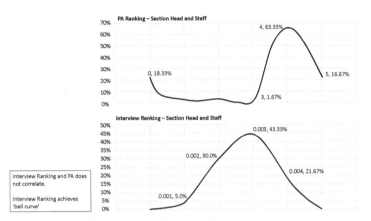

Fig. 5.7. Skewed Performance Appraisal Scores.

4. HR data are typically small data. To continue with the comparison with marketing analytics, the company can have a million customers. But it will not have one million employees. Best to not over-complicate or over-engineer data gathering and hypotheses testing. Statically speaking, we do not need perfect statistical models with very high correlations all the time because the data are small. An approximate answer will usually work: If the company can earn a dollar more today than yesterday, if it can save a dollar and improve an employee experience more than yesterday, then, we can say we have helped the business. Besides, it may be difficult to set up pilot tests and control groups – even in the sales incentive space. If it is possible, then by all means go for it. If it is not, then the analysis is all the more important and the HR analytics team, along with the stakeholders, can stand by the solution knowing that the data support it. That way, the focus becomes on appropriately implementing the solution and measuring the outcomes. If it works, great! If it is not as good as expected, change course immediately!

5. Be mindful that employee awareness can change their behaviour. A consulting firm found that when they told employees that there was a software installed in their computers that was monitoring their work, productivity doubled!

6. One key aspect about engaging in an HR analytics project is the kind of error that the stakeholders are willing to tolerate. This is generally best decided upfront: is a false negative better than a false positive? It depends on what is the bigger probability of an error. If the wrong person is hired that is a false positive. The employee was expected to be a good performer, and they end up not being so. A wrong hire can hurt the business, but not hiring the right person will never be known. Thus, in this case, a false negative is preferable, at least in practical terms!

QUESTIONS

1. In the case of the Indian Semiconductor Company described earlier, how would you have improved the model? What do you suggest can be done to have a more robust way to predict the turnover rates?

2. In the case of the Singaporean Bank, do you agree with the recommendations suggested? What else could you suggest management do to improve the Bank's results through individual performance?

3. In Fig. 5.8 which describes a performance measurement model, what observations and recommendations would you make to improve the analytical – and practical – usefulness of the model?[1]

---

[1]For instance, all job types have the same competencies and the same weight. Is this appropriate? Or should these be adjusted by job family and/or grade? Are 21 dimensions too many for evaluation? Or is more detail better? Should grading be a continuous model? Or best to use discreet scores? Should the target be 5 (which means all scores are 'discounted' from 5)? Or is it best to set targets at 3?

Competency Factor	Weight	Score	Target
Personality and Behaviour	**25%**		
Integrity	25%	4.50	5.0
Discipline	20%	3.90	5.0
Responsibility	25%	4.50	5.0
Communication	15%	4.10	5.0
Work Enthusiasm	15%	4.25	5.0
Job Presentation	**30%**		
Customer Service	20%	4.20	5.0
Technical Knowledge and Ability	20%	4.00	5.0
Efficiency and Effectiveness	15%	4.00	5.0
Contribution to the Team Success	15%	4.30	5.0
Follow-up to Action	15%	3.99	5.0
Implement Immediate Action	15%	4.10	5.0
Work Process	**20%**		
Timeline Work Management	25%	4.10	5.0
Reporting	20%	4.10	5.0
Work Creativity	20%	4.10	5.0
Management Tools and Work Environment	20%	4.10	5.0
Persuasive Skills	15%	4.10	5.0
Leadership	**25%**		
Planning	20%	4.25	5.0
Build Effective Teams	20%	4.30	5.0
Problem Solving	20%	4.00	5.0
Decision Making	20%	4.20	5.0
Supervising and Controlling	20%	4.20	5.0

Fig. 5.8. Performance Measurements – Case Study.

6

TRAINING AND DEVELOPMENT

CFO asks CEO, 'What happens if we invest in developing our people and then they leave us?'

CEO responds: 'What happens if we don't, and they stay?'

6.1 WHAT IS THE PURPOSE OF TRAINING?

According to Wayne Cascio, training consists of planned programs undertaken to improve employee knowledge, skills, attitude and social behaviour, so that the performance of the organisation improves considerably.[1]

More specifically, training seeks to improve one or more of the following areas:

- The productivity or the quality of the work currently being done

- The speed and number of promotions by preparing employees for a possible next level of work

---

[1]Wayne Cascio: Training Trends; Macro, micro and policy issues. *Human Resource Management Review*, 13 November 2017. Accessed online on 17 February 2019.

- The speed of change due to new strategies, products, technologies, merger or other new circumstances introduced into the workforce

- The speed to onboard newly hired or promoted employees (including lateral moves)

- The execution of work in terms of health and safety compliance.

There might be other objectives that training can help with, for instance diversity and inclusion, but for our purpose, the above-mentioned points will be enough to address training as an HR process where analytics can be of help.

Delving a bit deeper into this definition, we can think of the purpose of training as an investment the company makes, aimed at achieving better business results. As such, it is important to understand, from the company's perspective, if there is a positive return on this investment.

In this chapter, and in subsequent chapters, we will use an HR process – in the case of this chapter it will be training – as a means to delve into analytical concepts – in this chapter it will be ROI and Optimisation. Please note that this in no way means that the only way to analyse training is with these two approaches, nor does it mean that these two approaches only work for analysing training. There could, for instance, be a return on investment (ROI) on compensation programs, or on recruiting strategies. However, by illustrating different ways to address different problems, we hope the reader gains an awareness of possible approaches to tackle HR analytics problems.

6.2 WHAT IS RETURN ON INVESTMENT?

In simple terms (for a more complete understanding of this topic, readers are referred to financial theory books on this subject), return on investment (ROI) measures the gain or loss generated on an investment, relative to the amount of money originally invested. ROI is usually expressed as a percentage and is typically used to compare a company's profitability or to compare the efficiency of different investments (Phillips & Phillips, 2015).

The formula for calculating ROI is:

$$\text{ROI} = (\text{Net Profit/Cost of Investment}) \times 100$$

To put this notion in the context of training, assume a company spends $800,000 to train all of its manufacturing employees to produce more efficiently. As a result, the company later is able to reduce its wastage and thus improve the yield on the raw materials employed, with a savings of $2,000,000/year. The ROI can be simply calculated as ($2,000,000/800,000) $\times$ 100 = 250%. In other words, the company receives a benefit of 250% on this training investment. Not many investments have that high a yield!

In reality, calculating ROI can get more complex. For one, the savings on the manufacturing yield accrue every year, whereas the investment on training happens only at the beginning. In properly assessing the ROI of training, it is important to include the time element as well. To address this, finance uses the concept of Net Present Value (NPV), whereby the comparison is made considering the future savings as a difference in cash flow, discounted to today, using a discount rate which is often assumed to be the Weighted Average Cost of Capital (WACC) or other similar measures of the company's cost of money. This is done following the principle that money in the future is worth less than money today, and therefore $800,000 in savings three years from now is worth less than if you had that money today (think impact of inflation, or loss of investment income as a proxy). If you have an opportunity to calculate NPV as a means of determining ROI, the Finance folks will be grateful, as they tend to look at most other investments with the same lens.

However, this is not often feasible, partly because it is not always easy to separate the impact of training (or other HR programs) alone, on the savings achieved. Over time, there will be other improvements, such as new technology, new raw material, new production or quality assurance processes, etc. Over time, the effect of training is diluted with the effect of other investments. Thus, at a minimum, if it is possible to show a positive ROI on the year after the investment in training was made, this will be often enough to justify this and future similar investments.

6.3 OPTIMISATION

In an earlier chapter we discussed the concept of **Prescriptive Analytics**, which use optimisation and simulation algorithms to advice on possible outcomes to answer the question: '*What* **should we do?**' Prescriptive analytics aim to **quantify the effect of future decisions** to advise on possible outcomes, before the decisions are actually made. At their best, prescriptive analytics **predict not only what will happen, but also why it will happen**, providing recommendations regarding actions that will take advantage of the predictions.

Continuing on this line of thought, the next building block is optimisation. We can define optimisation as the search for the best and most effective solution to an analytics problem. Optimisation entails deciding how to best leverage limited assets, time and resources in situations with varying levels of uncertainty. Common prescriptive applications include staffing projects, determining budget usage, deciding to pursue a proposal, etc.

The main aspects of optimisation are as follows:

- **Segmentation**: Dividing up the impact of training programs based on demographic or other categorical data, to determine how the different groups respond. For instance, is training more effective for employees with more than three years of experience?

- **Mixture**: Breaking down training programs into multiple parts, to determine the ROI of each part, and how these parts can be combined to provide potential synergies and diminishing returns.

- **Saturation**: Looks at the amount of training in an organisation or for an individual, to find whether there is a 'tipping' point or threshold that needs to be crossed before the return is realised, or beyond which, no additional training yields additional benefits.

- **Metric Interaction**: Tests the relationship between the key performance indicators. For example, if training has positive impact on customer satisfaction, and this in turn has an impact on revenue per client.

- **Time Line:** Examines how performance changes over time; Some training programs may require some 'latency' time for results to kick in. Also, results may fade over time without follow-up training.

It is important, when carrying out HR analytics, to understand how these different concepts can be applied to better understand the data from an HR perspective. This can help achieve more insightful outcomes of the analysis and provide better results for the business. In the following sections we elaborate further on these concepts.

6.3.1 Segmentation

Recently, the head of sales for an office supply company was discussing with his HR Business Partner (HRBP) about the possibility of rolling out a sales training program which was touted as a success at boosting sales overall in another region. The HRBP wanted to train the entire sales force, but the head of sales was weary that this sales force was mostly new and eager to learn, whereas the more veteran sales reps would be reluctant to change old habits. He wondered if segmentation may reveal that new sales reps would benefit more from the training than seasoned reps. The HRBP argued that this may seem discriminatory, and thus they agreed on the following (note that this was a 'negotiated' hypothesis) ...

Hypothesis:
Training should be prioritised for the top performing sales force.

As part of the analysis, historical sales results were collected, and sales reps were categorised into five (5) quintiles: from the bottom 20% to the top 20%.

Both executives were eager to see the results of the study, each for their own reason. The analytics team was set to find an answer

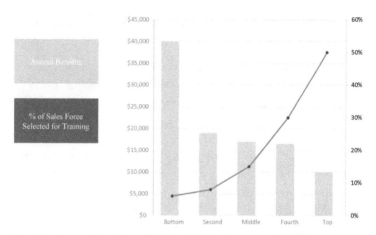

Fig. 6.1. Annual Benefits of Training by Performance Quintiles.

to the question 'Which group is generating more additional sales as a result of training?' The results are shown in Fig. 6.1.

It turns out that the lower performing sales reps, which in this case was highly correlated with the more senior reps, were increasing their sales results much more than the better performing reps. Had either executive prevailed in their views, without the intervention of the HR analytics team, the training program would not have been optimised.

6.3.2 Mixture

Many companies opt to spread their human capital investments, and training is no exception. Take as an example, the sales force training described earlier. Many companies choose to work with different vendors in providing training to the sales force, more on the basis of the vendor's reputation, or feedback from the trainees. Sometimes, an additional argument can be heard about having different vendors with different theoretical approaches, so that the overall effect is one of a 'rounded' training experience. But this theory fails to consider to what extent combining some elements, and not others, yields better results. With content available from a variety of providers, and many customised programs, the combinations of potential investments can become large.

When looking at problems of this nature, there are two important concepts to keep in mind: Synergy and Diminishing Returns.

1. **Synergy**: When two things combine into something more than the sum of the parts. For instance, classroom training provides theoretical groundwork and coaching provides practical implementation.

2. **Diminishing Returns**: When multiple items are combined, and the effect is less than the sum of the parts. Could be there is only so much improvement that can be attained, or there is overlapping content among different programs.

6.3.3 Saturation

This concept introduces the idea that the ROI may not be a smooth, straightforward calculation. Getting a return may require a certain threshold of investment to show any returns at all. But the effectiveness may taper off after a certain amount is invested. In training, for example, providing people with additional training may be effective, but at what point is maximum effectiveness reached?

For instance, in training bank tellers, how much product training is required before they can effectively sell a specific bank service? And how much training is too much?

6.3.4 Metric Interaction

Many analytic methods tend to focus on a single outcome, which is a narrow view as it does not consider the systemic nature of HR; that is, when impacting one part of the relationship between employees, their roles, and the customers, we often find that other parts are impacted as well. If we change the sales commission plan with no training to go with this change, we are likely to find a different result than if we couple the change of sales compensation with training to explain the new behaviours expected or the new products to be sold. Thus, when conducting HR analytics projects, it is necessary to consider how different measurements combine and interact.

Here's an example where metric interaction was an important decision point related to training in an insurance company's call centre:

- *Context*: Credit protection introduced as additional source of revenue; training used to teach effective sales behaviour to customer service agents

- *Hypothesis*: Training will increase sales of credit protection plan

- Training was inexpensive, therefore the company expected a high ROI

Was it a success?

- Call handling time showed a strong correlation with both sales and training

- Training led to increased call handle time, which was strongly correlated with sales; that was seen as positive until the increased cost due to extra time spent was considered

- Agents spent extra time selling the credit protection product, partly due to training, but mostly due to financial incentive

- However, sales of the product had a low success rate, and low profit

- The key question was whether the agents should have been selling the new product at all

In conclusion? No, not a success.

Keep in mind that, many times, results can be surprising and even counterintuitive. Remember that the role of HR analytics is not to confirm your, or the sponsor's idea. It is to provide evidence and insights to make better decisions.

6.3.5 Time Line

Often, there is a need to divide the data into more groups than just 'before' and 'after' the investment. One reason for this is that investments have varying degrees of 'Stickiness': A 'highly sticky' investment continues to offer benefits for a long time, whereas a 'less sticky' investment loses impact after a period of time. One example of 'less sticky' programs are technical training on things that change over time, such as:

- Sales training on the current year's model

- Equipment that fade as clients move to a new level of technology

The other side of 'stickiness' is lag time. Some training programs take time to show benefits, for example:

- Industries with long sales cycles often experience lag time

- If a program helps to fill the pipeline for products that take 18 months to close, measuring the effect after six months may lead to the wrong conclusion

6.4 THE ROI OF TRAINING[2]

6.4.1 Can Training Be Measured?

The reality of training in many organisations often looks like this: the employee goes for training and the company incurs cost both from the direct expense on the training and logistics, as well as the lost time while the employee is away from the job. After he completes the course, the employee returns to work with a binder, and promptly puts it onto the desk or a shelf, where it sits for a long time. This lack of emphasis on post-training in many organisations is part of the reason many line managers feel that training is unproductive. Some larger organisations might set quotas on training, for instance: 'every individual that works here must go through 40 hours of training a year'. These organisations would have many course options to choose from. Employees, on the other

---

[2]With thanks to Leong Chee Tung, CEO of Engage Rocket, who provided valuable input to this section.

hand, may consider these trainings as benefits, with the added bonus that they look good as resume builders.

No surprise then, that senior management is often tempted to slash the training budget: 'Let's remove 20% next year since nobody seems to care about training.' It is very tempting to make rash decisions like that without a thorough understanding of some of the real changes that training can do within the organisation. To address all sides in this scenario, HR analytics can support the HR function in figuring out how to deal with the reality of training, and how to deal with it intelligently. The aim is to answer the question: 'why are people too busy working to go for training', or better still: 'why should people go to training in the first place'?

Let us consider a typical example, where HR asks the business heads to send some of their employees to training. A typical reply would be: 'Is it really necessary? Why are we spending money on this?' HR would then normally answer something like: 'there's a gap here, so we need to fill it up' (unless we are talking about regulatory trainings, which are mandatory). The HR team would try to reason with the business heads, and generally the arguments centre about engagement or attrition, adducing that some people leave because they feel they are not being skilled enough, or not valued enough. These data come from exit interviews and from observations on the ground.

If HR succeeds with this line of reasoning, the line will respond along the lines of: 'Ok, we try training. We give it a go then we see how it works.'

Eventually, therefore, success of training is measured as a reduction of turnover or an increase of engagement. And this is as numerical as this discussion usually gets.

However, training is a business decision. If the business is going to allocate scarce resources into training, not just the money value, but the opportunity costs as well, there should be an expectation that the training will generate tangible, monetary results. The response from the business should be: 'Ok, tell me what I am getting out of it?' HR must articulate clearly why this is useful for the business, not just appealing to the emotional sense of 'we need to develop our people', but also explaining that the money they are putting into training will generate a return for the business.

What exactly does it mean to have an ROI on training? In addressing this question, we will compare two of the types of training, as described in Section 6.1 previously.

Functional training, broadly speaking, is role specific. For example, a software engineer will have specific software engineer training; a salesperson, will have specific training around sales processes or marketing strategies. **General training** would be concerned with things that are common to all jobs, such as leadership management, ethics, or regulations that have to be met. In general, it will be easier to calculate ROI on functional training than on general training, as one deals more with skills and competencies to perform the current role, whereas general training often is used to help in career development and thus has a longer-term horizon.

When we speak about Return on Investment for training, therefore, it not only has to focus on how much is spent on training and how much the business gets back in returns. In addition, to really measure return on investment, there is a need to measure transfer of training. If the employee learnt from the training, that is a necessary condition, but not sufficient. The skill or competency learnt must be transferred to what the employee does or achieves, and how he or she does it, in order for there to be a return.

This is an interesting perspective that adds depth, but also complications, to the job of the HR analyst. Results have to do with the application of the knowledge, not just the acquisition of knowledge. How to articulate that transfer into an equation?

If we follow the analytical process described in Chapter 1, one of our first tasks is to properly define the problem. Perhaps, before going through training, be clear about current level of knowledge of staff on the topic to be taught. Also, what is the change desired? This initial set-up will later allow for easier measurement of improvement and transfer to their work, either for functional or general training.

From strictly a financial perspective, this is very clean, as long as the time element is expressly considered, because there is a certain payback period to training. In other words, the question can be asked differently: 'If the business puts in a dollar and expects to get back $4.50, how long does it take for that $4.50 to come back? If it is expected to come back in 5–10 years, does it make sense to put in a dollar today?'

Another interesting question to address with regards to training is that HR not only has to convince leaders to send their people to the training programs, but also needs to convince the leaders to train their own staff. Typically, they would claim: 'No time. Too busy!' But what if HR analytics could show that when the line trains their own staff, the ROI is higher? On the one hand, it is true that line managers are busy working on their own KPIs, and that training can be outsourced to at least equally, if not more, capable trainers, at least skills-wise. And yet, on the other hand, it can be argued that, if it is the manager themselves doing the training, there will also be a tendency to have greater understanding of the issues, and that employees (and the boss!) will follow the process as taught. It might also make managers act more like coaches, and could save money in the delivery of the program. Of course, there may be naysayers that disagree with this premise, arguing that it would be best to contextualise the training in a format where the leader is not involved, in the sense that employees already go to their boss with some frequency. If they are also the trainer, there would be no fresh context. And battle lines are drawn, both sides wanting to impose their opinion. Another argument could ensue, that perhaps in terms of technical skills; the manager needs to do the training. That way, the manager would be able to communicate with his team as to what the new product or system is all about. For instance, a manager goes to meet a key client, who makes a request: 'I need this done.' If the manager has already trained the team, he would know how difficult (or easy!) it would be to deliver for the client, and what it will take to deliver successfully, and profitably. Or he could also know that the team does not have the necessary skill to adequately deliver this task for this client, and passes on the client's request.

The manager and the employees can understand, at least at an executional level, what is going on, why are the data going this way?

Perceptive readers will realise that these are competing hypotheses, subject to testing, to determine which approach would have the higher ROI. An HR analyst could ask the question: 'What training would benefit from having the leaders there, and what training wouldn't?' Instead of making it an all or nothing proposition, the analyst can seek common ground or a more definitive approach. The arguments can be turned into hypotheses; not a 'gut' belief. This is testable. How would you test it?

One way to test would be to determine the skill acquisition and application of employees trained by an internal leader on a specific skill, against that of another group of employees trained by an external vendor. Or perhaps involvement does not necessarily mean that the presence of the manager is required in the training, but more as an after-training coach. We can also study if that helps or not.

The point we make here, which is consistent with our approach to HR analytics, is to not assume that one side or the other is right, based on their arguments or HR's beliefs. HR analysts can define these opposite positions as hypotheses, and test them. The beauty of doing analytics is that HR, and the line managers in this case, no longer have to rely on their 'gut feel', even if it is based on prior experience. It does not matter if HR believes that this or that position is right or wrong. Instead, the HR analyst will take each one of them as a hypothesis and test.

To illustrate this point, let us think about how the CEO of a start-up company addressed this exact question.

The company had just hired a team of three salespeople, whose job it was to grow sales, replacing the CEO himself who had been running the sales area singlehandedly for the whole of last year. At first, he figured: 'I'm hiring these salespeople because they're smart, they're supposed to have a proven track record, they're supposed to know what they're doing. Should I spend any time at all training them?' As he stayed up late for several nights in a row, to prepare training material that distilled his knowledge into someone that was teachable and repeatable, he realised it was hard work! Why even go through that pain? He was tempted to just say: 'here's the script, here's our product, go read this and then in two weeks, come back with some sales.'

What made him change his mind and carry out the training, was something he read in the book 'High Output Management' by

Andy Grove.[3] In this approach, there is the start of an analytical process. He started with an assumption that the training would consist of four lectures that would last one hour each. And it would take about three hours to prepare each lecture. Then he made some simplistic and conservative assumptions on the productivity improvement that would come from the training: the sales force would only improve their productivity by 1%. Thus, the three staff amount to about 60,000 man-hours per year. Productivity would improve by 60 hours a year, and the time invested is 16 hours per year. With these assumptions, plus the fact that the expectation was to grow the team to 10 people, it was easier to make a case that he should go through and prepare the material and train the staff, even though his hours were worth between two to three of the staff's hours. By sketching out the problem like this, the assumptions still need to be tested, but the answer was very clear.

To test the hypothesis, once the implementation happens, he wanted to see if the productivity improvements had materialised, but also if the training package was sufficient – were four lectures enough? Maybe it required six lectures, and each one should take four hours to prepare and two to deliver. But mainly he wanted to know if, at the end of six months or one year, he had saved man-hours by forcing himself to train the new sales force, or, if he should stop. To do that, he decided to not train the next batch of sales-people and observe their output for the first six months. The results of this test gave him a firm answer within a year. There was reso-lution to it because there were data, because there was a model.

Let us look at another example. In this case, your CEO asked you, as the head of L&D for your company, about a particular program. He wants to know whether to invest $1.5 million on this fancy new program that a consulting firm is offering. It is a program about coaching, designed to help managers learn about their own strengths and how to utilise them, and also how to identify the strengths of their teams and how to optimise them. He has asked for your thoughts about whether or not to make that $1.5 million investment.

---

[3] Andy Grove: *High Output Management*, second Edition. Vintage Publishers, November 2015.

The first idea that comes into your mind is to figure out what kind of business outcomes does knowing your strengths lead to. You ask the consultant, and he tells you: 'Well, when your team knows their strengths, our method analysis shows that they're three times more likely to be engaged at work; we find that teams that used their strengths report six times higher satisfaction in life.'

Next you ask the consultant if they'd be willing to run a pilot or test it out on different employees. Maybe test it out with a single department and check with them after the training if there is any improvement. You want to confirm, based on the information that the consultant has given on what is supposed to happen, if it does happen in your organisation. You expect it will be easy to convince the consultant to run a pilot because, if it actually works out, then you are going to invest and buy. The consultant replies: 'Well, your competitors are already putting our training to work for them, and many other companies are lining up too. It looks pretty good so far. Not sure we can run a pilot for you, being we are so busy!'

You insist, as you feel that, given the large sum involved, you need to come up with at least a proxy to sell this program to the CEO. You ask the consultant if, in his opinion, in the next five years the company will see growth in productivity and revenue. The consultant replies that: 'My previous client got 300% return on investment on this. Their productivity soared after 6 months.' You ask if they can send you the Excel spreadsheet, which they happily do, masking all relevant information, of course. Nevertheless, you show it to the CEO, who sees it and comments: 'That's XYZ company. What do they know about training? They were in a bull market at that time.'

You decide to structure a pilot: $250,000 to be deployed in the first six months. The CEO says: 'Ok, tell me more, I'm listening.' To design the pilot, you know that the most important questions is what to look for. Choosing the department can make or break the decision, as many pilots have failed because they picked the wrong department. Best to have as random a sample as possible. You ask the line managers, but every department has an excuse for why they are different.

You finally decide to pick a pair of Directors or Associate Directors from each department, send only one of each pair for the training. You explain to the person who does not go that 'we're doing an initial rollout, so we're doing part of the department at one time while the rest goes about the usual business.' This allows a comparison between the person who went for the training and the other who did not: you don't compare department to department, you compare within the pair. You want to have a successful pilot so that you can secure the remainder of the budget.

With pilot design sorted out, the next step is structuring how to present the ROI because the consultants' financial models are going to be beautiful, since they are marketing material at the end of the day. So, internally the onus will be on you to create your own models.

The first step towards creating your own models is to calculate the cost of the investment, before you figure out the return on the investment, which you will determine from the outcome of the trial group. The cost will include, at a minimum, the fees paid to the consultant. There is also the time spent by the participants, which can be calculated by estimating the hours spent in training and in preparation, times a daily wage rate (annual compensation divided by number of working days in the year works well). There could also be an opportunity cost, that is, the amount of revenue 'lost' by virtue of the employees not producing revenue. A way to estimate it can be annual revenue derived by the employee divided by the number of working days in the year times the number of days to prepare and participate in the training program. In this case, you estimate that cost per manager is $2,000 per day each, 2 man-days for teaching them and one day to prepare; 20 managers for the pilot, and an opportunity cost of $4,000 per manager/day. This works out to a hefty $360,000. This is in addition to the $250,000 of consultant fees, and does not include other incidental expenses such as meals and lodging, plus room rental. Let's assume these to be $300 for hotel room, $100 for meals and $600 for average airfare per person, plus training room rental of $2,500 per day, and some $10,000 extra for incidentals. This adds up to an additional $40,000. The expected ROI of 300% over the consulting fees would be $750,000 of added revenue, which is only slightly above the total cost of $650,000, but at least enough to run the pilot.

6.4.2 The Kirkpatrick Model

The Gold Standard in measuring the impact of training was developed by Donald Kirkpatrick, from the University of Wisconsin. Kirkpatrick first published his model in 1959. He last updated it in 1998.[4] In 2016, his son, James, and James' wife, Wendy Kayser-Kirkpatrick, introduced the 'New World Kirkpatrick Model'.[5]

The Kirkpatrick model is widely used, primarily because it is relatively intuitive and easy to operationalise. The model comprises four levels: Reaction, Learning, Behaviour and Results. We look at each level in greater detail and explore how to apply it. Fig. 6.2 summarises the model.

The Kirkpatrick model is made up of four levels: Reaction, Learning, Behaviour and Results.

- Level 1, **Reaction**: what did learners feel about the learning experience? Was it enjoyable? Did they like the trainer? It is

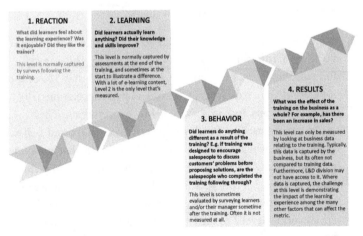

Fig. 6.2. Kirkpatrick's Four Levels.

---

[4]Donald Kirkpatrick, "Another Look at Evaluating Training Programs", American Society for Training, June 1998.
[5]James Kirkpatrick and Wendy Kayser-Kirkpatrick, "Four Levels of Training Evaluation", Association for Talent Development, October 2016.

normally captured by surveys following the training, which give an indication of the percentage distribution of participants liking vs not liking the course. Sometimes, it will also include weights of each of these responses, often ranging from -1 to 1; this weight is multiplied by the overall cost of the training. Assume that you gather these data for the pilot run and discover that 35% of the people loved the program ($x1$), 40% of the people thought it was so-so ($x0$) and the remaining 25% thought it was inadequate ($x - 1$). Using the cost estimated of roughly 650,000, the ROI, using this first level of Kirkpatrick, would be approximately $65,000 per year, which is basically 10% of the overall cost. Besides the fact that this is a low number, you do not think this is an approach that you want to take to senior management. However, as we have stated earlier, sometimes little or poor data are better than no data. As simplistic as this is, it is still better than not having any kind of ROI. In this case, the amount of return is not great, but you have some number to work with. You can say 'The first batch didn't work so well. Let's test again with the second batch and see if the number goes up.' This is one very rudimentary way of tracking the ROI on training.

- Level 2 is **Learning**. How much did the knowledge seep in? How much did participants understand the material? This can be done through tests. For example, a test may find that 5% of the population were excellent, 30% were above expectations, 40% met expectations and 35% were below expectations. These results can be used as weights ($1.50x$, $1.25x$, $1.00x$ and $0.50x$, respectively), which can be multiplied by the cost that has gone into the training. In our example, this approach would yield a return of $666,250 per year. Note that, in this case, the weights applied are completely arbitrary. In making a case using Kirkpatrick model level 2 to the CEO, it is feasible to say to him: 'For those who achieved excellent learning outcomes from this program, we've got 50% more than our money's worth; for those who are above expectation...', and so forth. The CEO, on the other hand, could comment that perhaps this is not convincing, as results may not mean that the people will be able to use this new skill over time.

- Kirkpatrick level 3 measures the change in **Behaviour** that comes from the application of training. This is interesting because there could be more than one way to measure the change in behaviour. For instance, one approach could be feedback from co-workers. This feedback could be gathered soon after the training, and later, perhaps six to nine months after, to determine if the change is sustained. Another creative way to measure change in behaviour is to put people in simulations. It may be the employee will not get many on-the-job opportunities to exhibit the new behaviour. Thus, if trainees go through a simulation, it could be possible to measure their behaviour change and also track their progress. Yet another approach could be to ask the trainee themselves, 6–12 months after the training, whether they think they have acquired the skill, and to what degree have they changed their behaviour? It is also possible to ask their supervisor, not just if the employee has acquired the skill, but if they have applied the skill, as seen through behaviour change in actual work circumstances. This assessment can also be done in the form of pulse surveys to the people reporting to the participants every month for as long as needed. This way it is possible to ascertain how long it takes for the behaviour to change, and for how long the change remains. Using this last approach as a methodology to determine ROI at level 3, let's assume that the data show 25% of participants have an average half-life of behaviour application of nine months, another 60% of participants have a half-life of four months and the remaining 15% did not show to have retained what they've learnt. The promised effects by the consultant were that the company would see an uplift of maybe a year. Using level 3, you estimate that a half-life of nine months would give you say an ROI of 1.5x; a half-life of six months gives you an ROI of about 1.0x; and a half-life of two weeks would give you 0.1. Applying these weights to the total cost would yield an ROI of about $643,500 per year, which is less than the total cost.

- Level 4 refers to **Results**. The data for this program, sometime after participants attended it, show than 20% of them saw improved profits of $400,000 on average; 50% saw no change or statistically insignificant change and the remaining 30% of them actually lost $200,000, on average. It is important also to attribute a certain percentage of the change in the financial situation to that training.

Armed with these calculations, you are now ready to build a business case to expand the pilot group: Should you go ahead with the rest of the $1.25 million? Under levels 1 and 2, and perhaps under level 4, it appears there is a marginal benefit. Under level 3, that benefit seems to not be there. In this situation, the ROI on this particular training looks low. You decide therefore to tell the CEO: 'We spent the initial money, but it does not seem we gained much from it; let's not spend anymore.' The caveat is that the Kirkpatrick model assessments can be very sensitive to the modelling assumptions. The robustness of the model can be tested through sensitivity. That is, tweaking some of the assumptions and then seeing the range of results obtained. If tweaking assumptions still keeps the model relatively robust, then there is greater certainty that, even after sensitivity analysis, it does not make sense to continue with this program.

One final consideration about the use of the Kirkpatrick model, or any other analytical model in general, is that it is important to weigh the cost of data collection and ROI calculation in itself against the benefit of knowing the ROI. If you are analysing a $20,000 investment and it costs $20,000 to collect data and calculate ROI, it may not be worth it.

SUMMARY

In this session, we have covered the purpose of training as a means to achieve organisational goals, and therefore susceptible to a measure, such as ROI. We also looked at how the various concepts of optimisation (Segmentation, Mixture, Saturation, Metric Interaction and Time Line) can be used to analyse training problems. Finally, we explored the Kirkpatrick model to calculate the ROI of training under four levels (Reaction, Learning, Behaviour and Results), which is a widely used approach in practice.

QUESTIONS

- Is it possible to estimate the ROI of training for all training programs? Which are more or less susceptible to this calculation?

- Is the Kirkpatrick model at levels 1 and 2 sufficient to justify an investment in training programs?

- A vendor is recommending a program to make supervisors better at 'dealing with difficult conversations' at work. How would you apply the concepts of optimisation and the Kirkpatrick model to set up an analytical approach to determine if it would be a good investment?

7

STRATEGIC RESOURCING

7.1 STRATEGIC RESOURCING

In this chapter we will turn our attention to Strategic Resourcing, sometimes referred to as Workforce Planning and, at the same time, learn various forecasting techniques.

Strategic Resourcing is one of the most interesting topics in HR because workforce planning gets at the heart of strategy formulation and implementation, from the HR point of view. When organisations think about future strategies, it becomes necessary to address how that strategy will be implemented through people. For instance, many organisations are worried about the implications of the Fourth Industrial Revolution (4IR). Will they need to retrench? Will the current workforce suffice? Our view is that lower-level jobs are at risk but there will be a need for more employees who can do the new jobs – so the net employment of any given company might actually remain neutral or go up. Perhaps we are still 5–10 years away from any meaningful (large scale) implementations of AI/Robotics. And yet, organisations need this on their radar and need to start thinking about how it might affect their business.

Empirically, there are two ways HR can approach this: one is to grow the business and then hire people to help manage it. Under this model, the HR department will put greater emphasis on recruiting. The other approach is to anticipate the growth in people given the expected growth in the business. In other words, if the organisation is planning on growing the top line, it should also be planning on how they will have the right number of people, in the right location, at the right time. Otherwise, the growth may not materialise.

7.2 IT ALL STARTS WITH BUSINESS STRATEGY

Understanding the organisation imperatives and the strategic intent is the logical place to start in the development of a workforce plan.

Recently, a supply chain company was looking to expand its business in Asia, specifically in China. The financial projections, backed by marketing data, suggested that the company could grow in excess of 23% per year – and potentially double its business in three years – given the growth in trade in the country, the positioning of competitors and the technological advantages the company had to offer. However, they had not included the people element in their plan, as it was assumed that 'HR would just have to find the people for us.' The problem, of course, came when the requests for people came to HR. In general, they were only to fill one in three roles in the timeline provided, and even then, at a premium of 20% or more over the average salaries of incumbents doing similar roles, all of which started to create a wave of dissent in the current workforce, which were now feeling both overworked, to fill the work demands for which there was insufficient manpower, and underpaid, as the new arrivals had higher compensation and yet lacked sufficient training and knowledge of the company's technology. Needless to say, the company did not achieve its aggressive sales targets, and had to go back to the planning table, this time to think through how they would plan for the workforce required and temper their growth objectives accordingly. The point to be gained from this example is that, although the company had great growth plans, these were definitely curtailed by their inability to implement their strategy due to insufficient people. This is why strategic resourcing is at the heart of what HR needs to do to be part of the strategic planning discussion.

7.3 WORKFORCE SUPPLY AND DEMAND

We stated earlier that the idea of strategic resourcing is to help organisations plan for their business growth (or change) by ensuring that it will have the people in the right number, doing the right job at the right time, in order to implement the business plan.

Strategic resourcing aims to identify the critical capabilities (organisational, leadership and technical) to achieve business strategy, to determine the employee skills needed to conceptualise, sell and deliver the firm's products and services, and to forecast how many people are needed to deliver the planned results effectively. In addition, strategic resourcing is also a useful tool to help conceptualise a flexible, agile workforce across the organisation, look for opportunities to align/change roles to reflect internal and external requirements, discover effective ways to build and attract talent and to optimally deploy critical capabilities and roles. By helping in this way to avoid capability gaps/risks, workforce planning's effectiveness can be measured by an increase in current workforce productivity and by evaluating how deployment choices impact service delivery and cost efficiency.

Strategic resourcing, therefore, is a pro-actively managed process. It is future-oriented, as it looks beyond the current-year horizon. It is a part of the business planning process, based on facts and figures of the critical workforce segments, and as such, it is owned by the business and driven/facilitated by HR, with support from HR analytics.

Note that, by implication, strategic resourcing is not reactive to current vacancies, nor is it a stand-alone, analytics-driven process. While it informs succession planning, it is not the succession plan, nor is it a workforce scheduling exercise. Finally, while it is a tool to forecast future people needs and how to address them, workforce planning is not a means of predicting the future.

Let us now look at the workforce planning process with an analytical lens. First is defining the business problem by gaining a better understanding of the concept of Right People. This means that employees have the capabilities that are needed to implement the strategy. Not just hierarchical level (how many managers and supervisors will be required), but also degree, or skills, that are specifically required. It also means that there will be enough employees with the right capabilities to run the new strategy. For instance, a retailer of high luxury watches, perfumes and similar high-end merchandise wanted to open 90 new stores in Asia over the next three years. When HR was notified of the plan, they began to search for both store managers and staff in some of the countries where there were competitors for luxury goods, such as China, Japan, Hong Kong and Singapore. However, the plan included the opening of nine stores located in Myanmar, Laos and Cambodia, where there were relatively few luxury retailers. Thus, it would be difficult to find enough people with the right experience and local language capability on short notice. Also, it was not feasible to send expatriates with experience in other markets, as the local language requirement was also an issue. However, they did think they could find enough prepared Burmese abroad, willing to return to Myanmar and 'hit the ground running' with limited training in the country they are found. In the end, they had to agree to postpone the plan to open stores in these markets until they had prepared enough managers to run them. And to prepare the managers, the company would hire them locally, requiring that they speak the local language and English and send them to English-speaking countries (e.g. Philippines, Malaysia) where they could be trained and redeployed back to their markets when ready. The key, in this case, was to understand what exactly it took to be able to do the job. They realised that, beyond the need for experience in managing luxury retail operations, it turned out that the critical skill was to be bilingual in English and the local language.

The next area where a better understanding is required relates to knowing when the new employees are needed. Staying with the same example, if the company determines that a pace of 30 new stores is how they envision the plan's implementation, it is possible to decide which are going to be opened first, and the recruiting team can get to work. But you will also provide input to the line managers in terms of available transfers and promotions, thus creating different vacancies. And although HR can influence the decision to delay the opening of the stores in Laos and Cambodia, it will still be necessary to hire there and fill a vacancy elsewhere with these staff.

The length of the delay in the opening of the stores in these countries being a function of the time it will take to recruit, transfer and prepare these local staff. This way of approaching staffing problems for growth is the embodiment of the idea of building versus buying talent. When needed staff are readily available in the market, the organisation may opt to buy talent and be less concerned with workforce planning. But, if the organisation has complex products and processes, or if the needed talent is not available, either because they do not exist or they are too expensive, then the organisation will nurture them from within, and workforce planning becomes critical.

In broad strokes, strategic resourcing involves making forecasts about the external drivers of change that match the organisation's growth plans. To do so, there are a number of assumptions, related to HR processes and policies, that have to be evaluated and included in the forecasting model. For example, one of them is how quickly can employees be trained to prepare them for new roles required. Another assumption that may need to be clarified is whether there is a way to change business processes, or introduce new technology, to decrease the number of employees needed in the future. Another important assumption to evaluate in making workforce forecasts refers to turnover rates: Is there a way to reduce the turnover rate so that not as many people leave, and therefore there are less people that need to be recruited and trained, thus shortening the time required to prepare them and the speed at which needed employees become available?

It is important to align workforce planning to the reality of HR practices and to the company's growth plans. If the workforce plan is done well, in many cases it will have as a consequence the need to change the organisation's growth plans to align it to the HR realities. This is what makes strategic resourcing so crucial because this is where the HR function needs to weigh in to indicate how likely the organisation is to succeed in the execution of the business plan, given the people constraints. This gets HR a seat at the notorious C-Suite table. And thus, the analytics behind the forecasting go beyond the statistical regressions. It is truly an understanding of what are the dynamics that need to be solved for to add the HR dimension in the firm's strategy planning.

One of the tools of strategy planning is building demand scenarios (see Fig. 7.1 below). Let's assume an example where, in one scenario (the likely outcome), revenue growth is about 5%, and a second, more optimistic scenario (the current stretch three-year plan), where revenue is expected to grow about 15%. The HR function needs to understand the implications, from a manpower planning perspective, of the outcome falling closer to one or the other scenario and be prepared in either case. In other words, from a HR point of view, is a 15% growth rate achievable? What will it take? If growth drops to 5%, will the organisation be able to align its labour costs? The implications of the workforce challenges and risks based on demographic patterns can be seen in the internal labour market charts we saw earlier, by analysing inflows, promotions and outflows of staff (Nalbantian, Guzzo, Kieffer, & Doherty, 2003).

However, to better identify the talent implications of the organisation's potential growth paths, HR analytics can help to examine the workforce structure and capabilities, and identify insights needed to implement the strategy.

HR's role is not necessarily to question the business strategy, but rather the ability of the company to implement that strategy. When doing strategic resourcing, the outcome should be an identification of future talent requirements, with utmost clarity around when and where should staff be placed – How many more people will be needed (talent demand – current staffing levels)? How many people are currently available, under the various planned-for scenarios, that the firm can 'build on' (talent supply – volume), and how long will it take to get the rest ready? What are the future skill

Driver	Scenario 1	Scenario 2
	Scenario 1 Description: **Pessimistic**	Scenario 2 Description: **Optimistic**
1. Revenue Growth	5% growth	15% growth
2. Technology Investment	Minimal change or spend	High change and large spend
3. Digital Adoption	Minimal adoption	High adoption
4. Competitor Activity	High investment in technology and digital adoption	Low investment in technology and digital adoption

Fig. 7.1. Examples of Scenarios.

requirements to achieve the strategy? How many people will the organisation need to hire if there's the probability that it will fall short with their build strategy? What drives demand for the critical workforce segments?

Where will this new needed staff be found? When should these be hired, in what job should they be placed, and will they be trained so that they will be ready when needed? Answering these questions analytically will allow the firm to determine of their current plans can be achieved, and the people/execution risks involved.

The firm may also want to consider other aspects that could potentially change the forecast. For instance, number and level of people expected to retire, changes to internal processes to achieve higher productivity (higher revenue or throughput per employee). For example, if revenue per employee today is $1 million per employee, and the firm finds a way to get that number to $1.1 million per employee, they will need 10% less people for the same amount of revenue in the future. The implication of this line of reasoning is that, when forecasting, it would not be correct to assume that for a certain growth in revenue, an equivalent rate of growth in people expense is required; the company may want to create different rates of growth for people, particularly if there are potential productivity gains available through changes in technology, tools, equipment or processes. In summary, manpower forecasting focuses on the supply of the workforce (recruiting, training and development, career planning) and applies workforce demand drivers (productivity, turnover) for each role to project future demand.

7.4 DEMAND AND SUPPLY GAPS

The outcome of this work are the gaps in terms of demand and supply, as well as recommendations around when to hire, what training plans to put in place and whom to train, when to promote, and how to reduce turnover. By having a clear plan around the 'inventory' of people and skills on hand compared to the needs in the future, it is possible to determine how much of a build or buy strategy needs to be put in place to achieve the organisational targets in the timeframe projected.

Recruiting is an important step in this process of closing the gaps. If it is possible to cover the supply immediately – with employees who can 'hit the ground running' – then there will be less of a need to train/develop staff. However, if supply is scarce, then the options may be to promote earlier in the career path and train/develop the staff to assume bigger roles later. Timing of recruiting and development must be aligned to the timing when the employee is needed. If it will take four years to develop a new recruit to the point where he can fill a needed vacancy, but the vacancy will be needed in two years, then this approach will not be enough. Another option is to accelerate the recruiting and promotion of internal staff, which may include promoting them 'ahead of time', provided they are given access to coaches, mentors and other means of helping them succeed, especially in the early going. Here is where productivity improvements and increased retention of staff are also part of the process, as the more people that are retained, the less people that are needed to hire. We refer the reader back to the internal labour market analysis explained in Chapter 3 (see Fig. 7.2).

How far into the future to forecast workforce supply and demand depends on how far into the future is the company's strategy plan. If different companies have a three-year plan or a five-year plan, then workforce forecasting needs to look at a three-year or a five-year goal, respectively. In cases where business plans

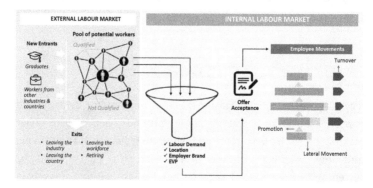

Fig. 7.2. Internal and External Labour Markets.

are longer than that (e.g. companies that have a very large capital expenditure base, like the oil industry for instance, tend to plan 10 to 15 years out), then the workforce plan needs to forecast that far off. Of course, the further forward plans are, the less visible things are. The longer the timeframe, the more it is that scenario planning can help.

Fig. 7.3 summarises the talent management options available to HR in developing the workforce forecast.

Let us look at an example of an education organisation that wants to build a new special education school. They expect that construction of the new facilities will take 30 months, and thus they need to have teachers and programs in place in 24 months, so that they can start marketing the new school and getting students enrolled. Their current plans call for 300 staff to run the school, including 100 new special education teachers. Currently, it takes four years to graduate with a special education degree, and their internal staff is not trained to handle special education students, which is too long for them to wait. What assumptions should they make? That they can find enough teachers in the market in the next two years? Or is it better to question the timeline of the strategy? In this case, HR may want to look at several options, including how many teachers can they realistically recruit from the market that are ready? How many that need one to three years of additional training to be ready? How many of their own internal staff can be accelerated through training to get them ready in three years? Will they need retention schemes to reduce turnover? Will all of these be enough to start the school in the three-year timeframe? If the

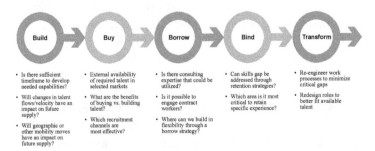

Fig. 7.3. Talent Management Options.

BASELINE NET INTERNAL SUPPLY
= Current Headcount - (Retirements + Terminations)

RETIREMENTS	TERMINATIONS
• Assume all employees retire at a given age (e.g. 62).	• Historical rates applied to current headcount, by segments (job grade, location, tenure etc.).
• Assume all employees retire at eligibility.	• Different models can be applied:
• Consider if different assumptions are needed for different employee segments:	– *Linear trend models*: extrapolate straight lines (e.g. if we lost 20% last year, we will lose 20% this year).
– Job Family	– *Stochastic models*: regressions to determine individual likelihood of leaving
– Hours worked	
– Physical limitations of the job	
– Age groupings	

Fig. 7.4. Forecasting Internal Supply.

answer is yes, then the plan can be implemented as devised. If the answer is no, then HR can influence the implementation of the plan by suggesting, for example, that not all grades open at the same time, or delaying the construction of the building.

Fig. 7.4 summarises the basics of forecasting internal supply.

7.5 FORECASTING TECHNIQUES

Forecasting is more than just a mathematical exercise. Simply taking the past growth rate and assuming that it will be the same growth rate into the future is usually quite risky because the forecast will extend the plan beyond the range of the data. There is no judgement applied in this case, and there is no plan as to how the forecast can be influenced to better reflect the needed outcomes. To increase the accuracy of forecasts requires a great deal of judgement, which is what makes forecasting the workforce a strategic competency.

7.5.1 Qualitative and Judgemental Techniques

One way to approach forecasting is to rely on the experience and intuition of the forecaster. This is particularly necessary when historical data are not available, or when predictions are needed far into the future. However, good forecasters know better than to rely purely on their own 'gut', and often use supplementary sources to complement their experience and intuition. Some of these techniques are as follows:

- Historical Analogy: this approach obtains a forecast through comparative analysis with prior situations

- Delphi Method: This method questions an anonymous panel of experts two to three times in order to reach a convergence of opinion on the forecasted variables.

Note that these two approaches can lead to very different points of view, which can then be translated into scenarios for planning.

7.5.2 Indicators and Indexes

Indicators are measures that are believed to influence the behaviour of a variable we wish to forecast. Indicators are often combined quantitatively into an index, a single measure that weights multiple indicators, thus providing a measure of overall expectation. For example, GDP measures the value of all goods and services produced in a country and, typically, it rises and falls in a cyclical fashion. Forecasting GDP is often done using leading indicators and lagging indicators. Leading indicators are those that change before the GDP changes, such as % change in money supply, formation of business enterprises, etc. Lagging indicators follow changes in the GDP, such as inventories on hand, prime rate, business investment expenditures, etc. From a strategic resourcing perspective, before being able to find more cybersecurity experts in the market, there should be an uptick in university graduates with this specialisation, and prior to that, more university programs offering this degree. Conversely, if GDP grows, the expectation is that wages will grow, and supply for talent will tighten.

7.5.3 Statistical Time Series Model

Forecasting via time series means using a stream of historical data, such as weekly sales, to predict what is likely to happen in the future. In fact, for many of our forecasting applications in HR, what happened in the prior periods will likely determine, to a large degree, what is going to happen, at least in the next few periods. In other words, when looking at a time series for the workforce, which is how staffing behaves over time, one of the biggest correlations of how staffing growth for next year, is staffing growth for the last year. That is to say, one of the biggest correlations to how many employees the company will have in the next year is how many employees the company has this year. We have to take into account that one of the best ways to predict the future is to use the data that we already have. So, how many senior engineers a company will have next year is going to be based on how many senior engineers it has this year. However, it is not so simple, and we do have to understand the trend patterns in the data. These can be caused for a variety of reasons:

- Random behaviour

- Trends (up or down)

- Seasonal effects

- Cyclical effects

Stationary time series typically have only random behaviour. In Fig. 7.5, showing the annual demand for manufacturing contract

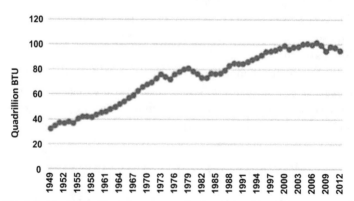

Fig. 7.5. Identifying Trends in a Time Series Annual Demand for Contract Manufacturing Workers.

workers, the graph shows a general upward trend with some short downward trends; in fact, it would appear that the time series is composed of several different short trends.

A seasonal effect is one that repeats at fixed time intervals, for example, after one year, month, week or day. This is illustrated in Fig. 7.6.

In this example, it can be noted that sick leave tends to happen mostly on Mondays and Fridays, and not on random days as you may predict in the absence of data. This is also true of things like sales trends, which can be affected by seasons (think Christmas shopping), or even by the weather (think of ice cream or soft drinks, both of which sell less on cold, rainy days). Another example of cyclical effects related to workforce forecasting and employment rate is how unemployment rate (think supply and demand for talent) is correlated to GDP and inflation (see Fig. 7.7). For us in HR it matters – because if there is a dip in the coming GDP, it will make supply of people greater. Conversely, if there's an increase in GDP, the company should consider putting things in place to make sure staff does not start to look for employment opportunities elsewhere!

7.5.4 Regression-based Forecasting for Time Series with a Linear Trend

Simple linear regression can be used to forecast, using time as an independent variable. Fig. 7.8 shows a linear regression model to

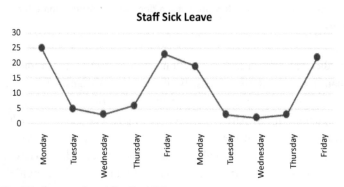

Staff Sick Leave

Fig. 7.6. Seasonal and Cyclical Effect.

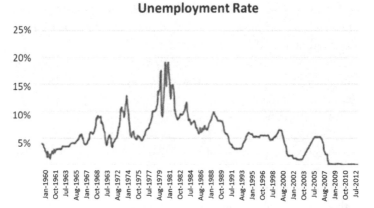

Fig. 7.7. Unemployment Rate.

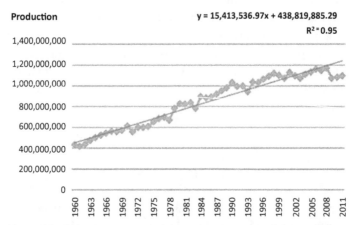

Fig. 7.8. Forecasting with a Linear Regression Model. *Note:* the linear model does not adequately predict the decrease in production after 2008.

predict manufacturing production as a potential indicator for manufacturing staffing needs. While this model seems robust (correlation of 0.95), we are not always certain of what else can be happening. In this particular case, the model seems able to predict within the range of the data but appears to be off past a certain point. Forecasting on a single variable (time) can be risky. To have a more accurate forecast, often a better option is to do a multiple regression.

7.5.5 Explanatory/Causal Models

In forecasting, other independent variables, such as economic indexes or demographic factors, may influence the time series. Explanatory/causal models, often called econometric models, seek to identify factors that explain the patterns observed in the variable being forecast. Let's look, for example, at Fig. 7.9. In this case, we are looking at an oil company's retail operation, which seems to be somewhat cyclical. If we use a linear model (the dotted line), it has a 0.68 correlation, or almost 50% confidence that the trend is there; the underlying data may be showing an approximate trend. Armed with this information, the company's HR department may decide to do one of two things: Change the recruiting policy to one where the company will staff for full-time employees up to the trough of the cycle, and supplement with part-time staff that are willing to work when needed. Or the company can choose to hire people at the peaks so that it always has people covering for customers. Which decision the company is likely to make would depend on how important it is to have full-time employees providing service at all times. If the company has a customer service strategy, it may choose to be on the high end of the curve and will justify the extra expense via increased customer satisfaction and retention. If it has a low-cost type of strategy, it will probably want to be on the lower end of the curve and save on salaries and benefits.

Predicted sales for week $11 = 812.99(11) + 4790.1 = 13,733$ gallons

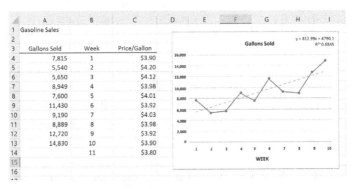

Fig. 7.9. Regression Forecasting with Causal Variables.

	A	B	C	D	E	F	G	H
1	SUMMARY OUTPUT							
2								
3	Regression Statistics							
4	Multiple R	0.920528528						
5	R Square	0.865883342						
6	Adjusted R Square	0.827555297						
7	Standard Error	1234.000219						
8	Observations	10						
9								
10								
11	ANOVA							
12		df	SS	MS	F	Significance F		
13	Regression	2	68974748.7	34487374.35	22.590239	0.000883465		
14	Residual	7	10683497.8	1526213.972				
15	Total	9	79658240.5					
16								
17		Coefficients	Standard Error	t State	P-value	Lower 95%	Upper 95%	
18	Intercept	72333.08447	21969.92267	3.292368642	0.013255255	20382.47261	124280.6963	
19	Week	508.6681395	168.1770861	3.024598364	0.019260861	110.9935232	906.3427669	
20	Price/Gallon	-16463.19901	5351.082403	-3.076611001	0.017800405	-29116.48821	-3809.877876	
21								

Fig. 7.10. Results of Multiple Regression Model.

However, the linear model may not be accurate enough in this case to make that kind of decision. For instance, it may very well be that the changes in price/gallon each week could be influencing consumer sales. We can say that average price per gallon is a causal variable and incorporate it into our regression forecasting model. By doing so, we can create a multiple linear regression model to predict gasoline sales using both time and price per gallon. Fig. 7.10 shows the results for the multiple regression model, with an r^2 of 0.87, which provides greater confidence when deciding on employment patterns.

$$\text{Sales} = \partial + \beta_1 \text{ Week} + \beta_2 \text{Price/Gallon}$$

$$\text{Sales} = 72333.08 + 508.67 \text{ Week} - 16463.20 \text{Price/Gallon}$$

7.6 CONCLUSIONS

By taking a longer-term view of workforce needs, organisations have at their disposal a larger set of potential people strategies. With appropriate HR analytics on hand, companies should be better able to:

- Identify where current internal talent pipelines will not be sufficient and adjust recruiting strategies as appropriate.

- Examine potential succession gaps and devise strategies where training and development programs need to be expanded.

- Influence annual career discussions by providing information about future roles where a shortage has been identified.

- Develop new external candidate pools by, for example, improving value proposition and employer brand through specific targeting.

- Move good performers in surplus areas to areas where a future shortage is expected, rather than making them redundant.

- Redesign work so that it can be completed by employees with different qualifications and experiences, or part-timers.

- Change the location of where the work is done to have access to the right talent.

It is often the case that the nature of the workforce gap will inform potential solutions. And if there is no apparent solution, perhaps the company can consider whether the business strategy needs to change.

Let us go back to the earlier example about building a special education school and the considerations about staffing. It could be that, after running the numbers, it becomes necessary to think things through because it could lead to a change in what numbers may look like. Let's assume that the organisation looks for available teachers and it seems like there are plenty of available teachers. The school may then want to apply the logic that it only wants teachers who are interested in special education as a profession. It may also decide that it does not have to overpay teachers because they are able to hire them, as they are keen to work in this environment anyway. The subset thus becomes different: focusing only on teachers that want to be special education teachers. Note that the subset becomes smaller, but the success may be higher. That is, it could be that only 20% of the available pool of teachers would like to work as special education teachers, and the success rate among these is a hiring rate of 50%. By focusing on this smaller subset, the school can lower its recruiting costs, reducing hiring time and a greater probability of success.

HR analytics, when applied to strategic resourcing, is most useful when it can inform the impact the HR function can have on the outcome, depending on the assumptions that go into the forecast. For instance, is there a better way to source for employees? Which is the best profile of staff to target? How quickly can they be trained to prepare them to be productive/ promoted? What are the best tools for staff retention? What is the best mix of full-time to part-time employees? Strategic Resourcing is more than estimating future employee needs; it is about changing the way processes work to increase labour productivity. Every assumption that goes into the forecast can be used as a guide to help think through what the things in the forecast are that can make it work for better for the organisation. It does not entail complicated maths. It is much more about the HR logic and thinking that goes into it.

SUMMARY

In this session, we have given an overview of workforce forecasting, starting from the business strategy, through the people strategy and planning, forecasting tools and techniques, to the outcome of the forecast exercise which is twofold: Better plan for resourcing of future business needs, but also better implementation of HR policies and programs to ensure the supply of staff meets demand in the right numbers, right quality of talent and right time.

CASELET: FORECASTING SPECIFIC TALENT NEEDS AT A NATIONAL LEVEL[1]

This prominent Singaporean public sector agency was responsible for driving a strategic national initiative and achieving its goal in 10 years. In order to plan appropriately, the agency wanted to

---

[1]With thanks to Siddharth Mehta, who provided great insights to this section.

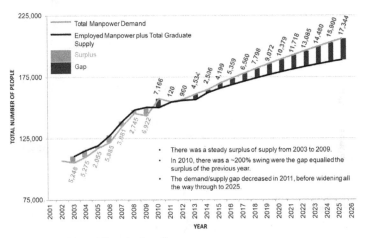

Fig. 7.11. Demand/Supply Gap Summary.

determine if there is sufficient workforce to drive that vision. So, in 2015 they embarked on a project to forecast the countrywide gap in supply and demand in the IT industry sector for the next 10 years.

The problem statement was to test, across the target sector, which are the functional areas that are likely to grow, likely to decline and likely to remain flat. Functional areas were defined in terms of the sub-areas of the IT function, and categorised as 'Infrastructure', 'Data Science', 'Software Application' and 'Cyber Security' (Provost & Fawcett, 2013).

The initial analysis of the aggregated demand–supply gap up to 2009 (see Fig. 7.11) showed that there was a surplus in these jobs; but for every year beyond that, the graphs show that there will be a deficit of that workforce, at an aggregate level.

This initial analysis also pinpointed which were the most rapid growth functions, and which are the functions that are likely to decline (see Fig. 7.12). That initial analysis showed that:

- The most aggressive growth rate can be seen for the Cloud Computing job family due to the current base number being small.

- Security Design and Engineering roles are forecast to increase ~2.5 times from 2015 to 2025.

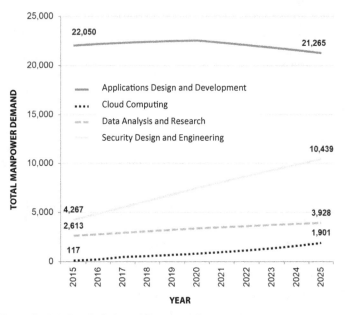

Fig. 7.12. Job Family Demand Forecasts Summary.

- Although increasing, the relatively conservative growth forecast for Data Analysis and Research reflects the immaturity of the function and lack of refinement around what constitutes a Data Scientist role.

- Demand for Applications Design and Development is forecast to remain flat through 2025. While the skills required in this job family may evolve, manpower demand will remain unchanged.

The HR analysts initially decided to use the causal approach – instead of time series – because they wanted to be able to understand what the factors are (cause and effect relationships) that drive the answers they would come up with.

With the strategy, the current situation and the business problem correctly stated, the next step was to think of the possible hypotheses. One hypothesis was that the IT industry, because it is such a prominent part of the economy, contributes significantly to the GDP. If GDP is projected to grow rapidly, that is an indicator that more people are probably needed in the IT sector. But it is difficult to make such a straight-line correlation, and the analysts realised they did not have enough data. Besides, Singapore, as an IT hub for the region, may have people hosted in the Singapore office that may be servicing markets outside of Singapore. So, it may not be possible to capture both the domestic and the international growth rates of these organisations.

Thus, the team resorted to the time series approach, focusing on past data trends and forecasting these data forward. The trade-off was that it may not be possible to know the causes for the projection.

The team thus felt the need to ascertain the strength of the model. To test the accuracy of a model like this, it is possible to use standard error (i.e. look at the true value and the estimated value, and the difference between the two is the standard error).

The team ran some initial models, and the naïve model predicted workforce demand with just a 1.43% error, which should mean that it was the best model. But the team was not satisfied, as they felt that the model was simply predicting the last value and keeping it constant through the forecast period years (see Fig. 7.13). The

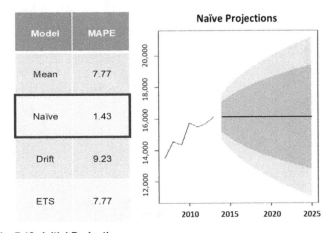

Fig. 7.13. Initial Projections.

projected values are represented by a flat line, which they felt was not a sensible one, and decided to seek more data to make their predictive model stronger.

The analysts went back to the public agency to secure more data with the hope to build more complex and revealing models that may yield better estimates. They ended up creating multiple models and were now confronted with a model choice decision. Their two best models were equally good and within a small range of error – one at 2.64% error rate and the other at 2.19%.

In order to make the right choice, the team went back to domain experts and interviewed them to understand their insights about the two models. One of these models (see Fig. 7.14) had a somewhat damped effect and it flattened after a point in time in the future. This was an odd prediction and suggested that, while the hiring would ramp up initially, it would flatten out after a point in time (the flattening of the curve). So the team went back to interview people in the industry to understand from them what they thought would be the hiring rates for different jobs, and to validate if their model was aligned with these experts.

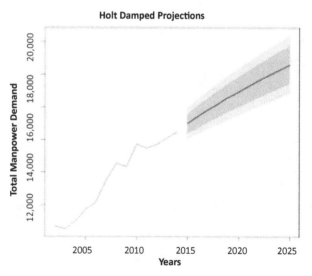

Fig. 7.14. Final Projections.

What the team concluded was that, as much as the sector is growing, technology is getting better and hence productivity is growing as well. Therefore, the workforce does not need to grow at the same rate as it did in the past during the ramp-up period. This confirmed the flattening of the curve in the future time-period. The model was predicting well, and the added interviews provided the necessary insights to make sense of this projected growth pattern. The team decided to select this as their model of choice (even though its error rate was slightly higher than the earlier model).

QUESTIONS

1. Determine the number of available actuaries in your market.

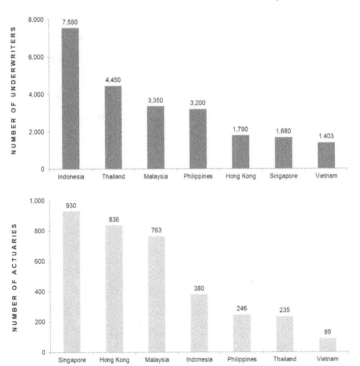

'Underwriting' information can be extracted from LinkedIn or occupational/industrial employment compositions of the market.

If using LinkedIn, look for the number of subscribers with 'Underwriting/Underwriter' in their job title.

To use occupational/industrial employment compositions, examine the % of underwriters in a country with a mature insurance industry (e.g. in the USA, underwriting occupation is approximately 5% of the total workforce in the insurance industry).

Assuming we are trying to determine the number of actuaries in Thailand, we can assume a similar composition % of actuaries in this market, and thus estimate there are 4,450 underwriters available in the country.

'Actuary' information can be extracted from actuarial societies' membership.

In Thailand, 235 members were registered under the Society of Actuaries. The majority are ordinary members, 36% are classified as 'Fellow' (which is the highest designation), followed by 9% of 'Associates'.

Hence, we may assume that 107 qualified actuaries (fellow and associate) are available in the market.

8

RECRUITMENT

In this chapter we will turn our attention to the application of HR analytics in recruitment while, at the same time, reviewing some important concepts about the basics of sampling methods.

Analytics in recruiting focuses a great deal on assessments: assessment testing, assessment centres, interviews, sussing out candidates both internal and external as well as development. To illustrate this point, it is worth looking at the case of a large financial services multinational company which was trying to determine how to hire the best possible sales staff. Up until that point, the firm operated under the belief that employees with good grades who come from highly ranked colleges would make good performers, and thus, their recruitment, selection and promotion processes were based on recruiting individuals who fit these academic drivers.

The HR analytics team went to work to determine if there was a correlation between good sales performance and these selection criteria. What they found was that the correlation was weak; where the candidate went to school, what cumulative grade point average (GPA) they had, the quality of the referees, these things did not make much difference in predicting their sales performance once they joined the company. The HR analytics team went to work to determine what the characteristics were of the top performing salespeople. What they found surprised them. Interestingly enough, having a grammatically correct resume was a predictor that an individual can sell well. Having completed some educational degree, any degree, and at any institution, also made a difference. Having sold high-priced products before, and done it well, was also highly correlated with future performance. One last characteristic found to be significant was the ability to work under unstructured conditions. These were the few factors that correlated to future sales performance in this company in the markets in which they operate.

8.1 HR ANALYTICS IN RECRUITMENT

In its simplest form, HR analytics can help to track the efficiency and effectiveness of the recruiting process. For instance, what is the cost per hire? Does it vary by channel (e.g. recruiting site vs agencies?). How about the quality of the hires: does it also vary by channel? If so, can any insights be drawn in terms of cost-benefit per recruiting channel? How diverse is the workforce in relation to the hiring pool? The efficiency of the process can be measured in terms of the time to fill jobs, and the number of new hires vs internal promotions for all non-entry-level jobs.

HR analytics can also use data to assess potential candidates and improve the probability of a successful outcome of the recruitment process. There could be a whole host of reasons that make a new employee good. If these reasons were universal, as it is often assumed that a person from a good university is better than a person from a not-so-good university, and that a new graduate that has an 'A' average in his university courses is better than another that has a 'B' average. As long as there are assumptions like these in the recruiting process, then deciding whom to hire should be easy: only recruit from the top universities and only recruit people who have an 'A' average, and voila! But in reality, that may not be the right answer and HR analytics can help find better answers than that.

In a typical recruiting process, candidates are chosen from a batch of CVs received, based on hiring criteria specified as requirements to perform at the job for which they are applying. The candidates are then asked to attend interviews by HR and the hiring manager, which, at best, are entrusted to assess 'fit' and 'technical skills', respectively. More often than not, there are no clear guidelines for selecting the 'right' candidate and, in fact, there is no consensus *beforehand* about what the way would be to identify and choose the best candidate. However, the recruiting process is akin to a manufacturing process, where the inputs are the candidates, the throughput is the recruitment and selection process, and the outcome is a quality employee (defined, for example, as an employee with a high probability of staying with the company for at least three years and with at least an 'on target' performance appraisal for this period). By reframing the process this way, we can apply analytics to identify which group of employee characteristics can yield a higher probability of a quality hire. More specifically, recruitment analytics can create value in two main ways: Employee Profiling and Segmentation, and Employee Loyalty Analysis to help determine if a new recruit will both succeed and stay.

8.1.1 Employee Profiling and Segmentation

Recruitment analytics can be leveraged for effective talent management by accurately profiling and segmenting employees. Data (including traits, behaviours, skills, experience etc.) can be used to profile 'what success looks like' in a particular role. The knowledge and insights extracted from this segmentation process can be applied to effectively classify candidates and automate the screening process.

For instance, predictive hiring tools can be developed by creating recruitment profiles based on the current company high performers. In other words, it is possible to identify success profiles, based on skills and behaviour traits, which are unique to each company as these profiles would be based on internal performance data. The aim of a predictive hiring tool is to increase the likelihood that every recruit will be a potentially well-performing employee by estimating their probability of success relative to the internal benchmark performance profile.

Note that it will be necessary to build a data set that comprises more than one type of information. The recruitment data set may include behaviours, as well as personal values, along with factual

Fig. 8.1. Probability of a New Hire Falling into Each Performance Quartile – Current Process vs New Process.

data like distance from home and grades. Thus, there will need to be more than one means of obtaining the data, which may consist of more than one tool (say, one for behaviours and one for values, at the least). These tools need to be standardised (that is, every candidate needs to go through the exact same process), as otherwise, the validity of the tests can be questionable.

Let's illustrate this concept with an example. In the current – traditional – hiring process, this company has the same chance of selecting a first quartile performance as a fourth quartile performer. By using a predictive hiring tool, the company can reduce the probability of a new hire falling in the first performance quartile. The aim is to focus on the possible performance variance spread (first quartile performers vs fourth quartile performers) and the potential attrition risk given the assessed characteristics derived from analysing current successful employees, with the objective of replacing poor performers with better performing new hires and, simultaneously, reducing the probability of high performers being replaced with new hires with lower monthly sales (see Fig. 8.1).

8.1.2 Employee Loyalty Analysis

Predictive models of analysis can also help in identifying loyal employees and to estimate the risk of attrition of each employee, to prevent the attrition of high-performing employees. HR analysts may explore behavioural data, along with data on demographics, performance, compensation and benefits (internal and external), rewards and recognition, training, and employee engagement survey results, to determine if there are patterns in how these characteristics combine to increase the probability of turnover (see Chapter 5 on turnover). Remember that some of the characteristics linked to loyalty may be related to distance from home, etc., which do not require tools to assess, but need to be included in the analysis as well.

8.1.3 Use of Gamification in Recruiting

Many organisations are less able to generate enough interest in their company to guarantee enough supply to their recruiting process, and thus a better pool of candidates to choose from. They may not have enough visibility of their company or jobs, as the market competition for new employees can, and often does, default to those companies with bigger brands or budgets. This can translate into a lack of continuous, strong pipeline, too many or ineffective sourcing channels and insufficient quality/diversity of candidates.

Another common situation, especially in smaller, fast-growing companies, is the need to quickly assess candidates without taking too much managerial time.

Additionally, many managers have both conscious and unconscious interview biases, are subjective in measuring potential and have varying levels of accuracy (and rater error) in assessing candidates with transferrable skills.

HR analytics has allowed for the use of gamification to provide a data-driven approach to make informed recruitment decisions.

Using the predetermined, unique company traits identified, the current employees play a decision-making game and patterns of responses are observed. Candidates are later screened into the recruitment process based on gameplay, rather than their previous experience and/or background. The results, via comparison to the response pattern of successful current employees, can be used to evaluate candidate traits in assessing fit and potential for a position. This process can help to quickly and accurately assess and rank candidates, while providing a more engaging experience for candidates.

In summary, HR analytics uses cognitive and emotional traits, not just resumes, to predict person and job fit. The process looks roughly like this:

1. Identify target candidate pool for assessment.

2. Identify 30–50 existing successful employees to set profile baseline.

3. Develop benchmark performance profiles of roles and flag high performers.

4. Current employees participate in assessments/games and responses/patterns are recorded.

5. Validate models developed.

6. Candidates participate in assessments/games and are ranked by fit with high performer model.

Note that, as indicated, the probability of ending with a good hire increases, to a point, with the number of tests. Interviews, assessments, data analysis, each by themselves may only give you a 50% probability, but the combination of the several tests may push the overall probability to over 70%. This is already a marked improvement over interviews alone!

By virtue of these combined results, the recruiter may end up with three candidates with a probability of success between 72% and 74%. Then, the recruiter can introduce these candidates to the hiring manager with the notion that – at that point, any of them has an equivalent chance of success.

Before continuing, we should take time to provide enough background on statistical sampling, which will be useful in doing analytics for recruitment.

8.2 BASICS OF EMPLOYEE SAMPLING METHODS

8.2.1 Sampling Plans

Sampling is the foundation of statistical analysis, whereas a sampling plan is the approach to be used to obtain samples from a population prior to any data collection activity.

A sampling plan should include:

- Objectives
- Target population
- Population frame
- Procedures to collect data
- Statistical tools for data analysis

The following example will help understand these concepts. A company wants to know how managers might respond to a leadership program:

- *Objective*: estimate the proportion of managers who would join the program
- *Target Population*: managers with less than two-year tenure in position
- *Population Frame*: managers who graduated from Singapore Management University
- *Procedure*: email link to survey or direct-mail questionnaire
- *Statistical tools*: summary of data by demographics and estimated likelihood of joining

There are two basic methods for sampling: Subjective and Probabilistic. Subjective methods can be broadly divided into two approaches:

- Judgement sampling: expert judgement is used to select the sample
- Convenience sampling: samples are selected based on the ease with which the data can be collected

Most probabilistic sampling, on the other hand, is often categorised as simple random sampling, whereby items are selected from a population so that every subset of a given size has an equal chance of being selected.

It is important to always remember that samples are subsets of the total population, and not the total population. Therefore, a sampling (statistical) error is inherent in any sampling process, which can be minimised, but not avoided. A non-sampling error is said to occur when the sample does not represent the population well. This usually results from poor sample design or low data reliability.

8.2.2 Sampling Distributions and the Central Limit Theorem from an HR Analytics Perspective

The sampling distribution of the mean is the distribution of the means of all possible samples of a fixed size n from a given population. The standard deviation of the sampling distribution of the mean is called the standard error of the mean. As *n* increases, the standard error decreases – larger sample sizes have less sampling error.

The Central Limit theorem states that, ideally, if the sample size is large enough, then the sampling distribution of the mean can be said to be approximately normally distributed regardless of the distribution of the population, and with a mean equal to the population mean. If the population is normally distributed, then the sampling distribution is also normally distributed for any sample size.

However, in HR analytics world, we should not so readily conclude that data are normally distributed, despite the central limit theorem. The reason is that, for most of what HR does, the data are generally skewed. Take, for instance, the most vaunted 'normal distribution' of all, the forced ranking in performance management. To be truly normally distributed, the tails on both side (significantly above target and significantly below target) would have to be equal; yet, this is generally not the case, as we often find more better performers than worse performers. This is because we systematically seek to eliminate poor performers from the company and retain good ones. Thus, the data are skewed. Even in sales compensation, we seek to do the same, so the central theorem is likely to fail as well since the population is not normally distributed to begin with.

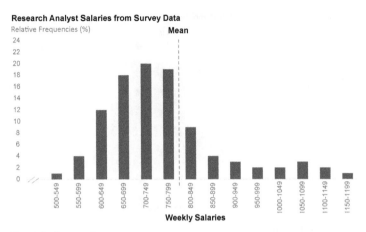

Fig. 8.2. Survey Data.

Fig. 8.2 shows how market data are generally also not normally distributed. There is significant variation in the data, and they are skewed to the right (notice the position of the mean vs the bulk of the data). In fact, it is often the case that these data are bimodal (or nearly so), as many companies choose to set their pay philosophy at the median of the market, and yet many others set it at the 75th percentile of the market, while not many would set pay at the 25th percentile. Besides, in the market there is often a 'minimum' (e.g. starting salaries for recent university graduates), but the maximum may be several standard deviations away. In addition, as employees get promoted, the salary data tend to have a heavier weight on new employees than experienced ones. In all, we systemically skew the data.

We could also look at company data (Fig. 8.3), which show that there is less variation compared to the market data graph (it is more symmetric). However, we cannot conclude that it is normally distributed (bell-shaped).

8.2.3 Confidence Intervals

A confidence interval is a range of values between which the value of the population parameter is believed to be, along with a

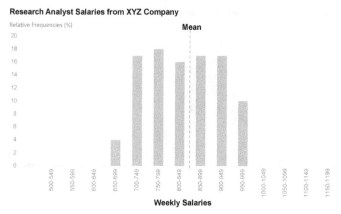

Fig. 8.3. Company Data.

probability that the interval correctly estimates the true (unknown) population parameter. The level of confidence is usually expressed as a percentage; common values are 90%, 95%, 99%. For a 95% confidence interval, if we chose 100 different samples, leading to 100 different interval estimates, we would expect that 95% of these samples would contain the true population mean.

Related to the concept of confidence intervals, is the notion of the 2-Sigma and 3-Sigma rules. These rules apply to any distribution and, as we have already made the case that in HR analytics most distributions are not bell-shaped, they can be applied in all cases we may want to look at.

- 2-Sigma Rule: At least 75% of the points in the data set will always be within 2 standard deviations from the mean

- 3-Sigma Rule: At least 88.9% of the points in the data set will always be within 3 standard deviations from the mean

Note that, for a normal distribution, the equivalent 2-sigma (z-score of 2) and 3-sigma rules would yield approximately 95% and 99% of the points to be within the range, respectively.

8.3 PRACTICAL FRAMEWORKS FOR USING HR ANALYTICS IN RECRUITING[1]

8.3.1 Three Levels for Analysing Talent

In this section we introduce a useful framework (see Fig. 8.4) to analyse talent, which is widely used by successful recruiting firms, such as DDI. The first level of understanding, from an HR analytics perspective, is what is the *current status* of the job market. The HR analysts can focus on questions such as: Is there high availability/ demand for specific roles? Is there a high demand for local employees, or do companies prefer to hire foreigners? Are there enough people graduating with the degrees sought?

The next step in this model is to start looking into *insights*. When bringing someone into the organisation, it is important to consider if the firm is going through some sort of transformation. That is to say, either being faced with a significant challenge, it is doing things differently than in the past, or is in the process of shifting gears to adjust to recent market changes. If this is the case, it is highly likely that the characteristics needed for new people may not be the same

SIGHT - What is the current status
• ... of the job market?
• ... of our talent?
• ... of the educational program(s)?

INSIGHTS - What changes have occurred that
• ...impact on our talent?
• ...impact on our business?
• ...impact on our operational risk?
• ...have we accurately identified potential risks?

FORESIGHTS - What can we expect in the future?
• Will we have the talent we need in the future?
• What adjustments will help get the most out of our talent investments?

3 Levels for Analysing Talent

Fig. 8.4. Three Levels for Analysing Talent.

---

[1]With thanks to Desmond Tan from DDI International for invaluable input to this section.

as those for current successful staff. This is important to note, as many organisations want to change in order to be more effective, and yet they continue to recruit the same people with the same profile as before. Senior management often expects people that come through the door to be exactly like them: They believe in transformation, but they do not always realise that, in terms of recruiting, they have to change their mindset: If the company wants to transform but keeps hiring the same people, it is not going to transform. The HR analytics team can help determine a better hiring profile, as was the case of the multinational financial services firm at the beginning of this chapter. Another area where HR analytics and recruiting profiles may be of assistance is in assessing employee risks, including the relationship between background checks, employee characteristics and risk mitigation. Although it is important to point out that, as in other aspects of current characteristics vs future behaviour where we are dealing with probabilities, assessments can help to minimise risk, but it can never eliminate risk.

The third part of this approach is *foresight*. Foresight means trying to determine what employee profile will be needed in the future, not what is needed now. Too often, recruiters are tasked to 'fill the vacancy', that is, to hire someone to fix what's broken now: 'I need this certain skill set to address this current problem'. Without consideration of what will be needed in the future, executives may find that once the thing that needs fixing is fixed, they don't actually need that skill anymore. HR analytics can help to look into the future to decide what profile is needed for now and later. Diversity of staff is another aspect that is becoming more and more important: not just in gender, but in age, in thinking, etc. HR analytics can help in determining the right mix of diverse teams that tend to do better.

8.3.2 Hiring Formula

Another useful model for HR analytics to frame recruiting decisions is to refer to the following hiring formula:

$$P\&A \times B\&C \times K\&E \times MF = \text{Performance on the Job}$$

where:

- P&A → Personality and Attributes
- B&C → Behaviours and Competencies
- K&E → Knowledge and Experience
- MF → Motivational Fit

In this formula, the first main criteria are personality and attributes – who the candidate is and how this may impact their success on the job. For instance, when recruiting for a highly hierarchical company, where entry-level tasks are simple and volume-driven, it may not serve to recruit individuals who are very talkative and enjoy socialising. Will this type of candidates be successful in this environment? Unlikely. Chances are they are going to be frustrated and may end up leaving the business on short notice. Knowing what type of personality and attributes drive on-the-job success is an area where HR analytics can help.

Next is behaviours and competencies – what is the candidate capable of doing, their skill set, coupled with their knowledge and experience, what they know. Note that knowing and being able to do are two very different things. One very simple example: A person can do a search on YouTube on how to do a brain surgery and learn all the steps in the right order. Can they proceed to put a patient under anaesthesia and perform the surgery? Not likely, they don't have the skill, even if they have the knowledge. This aspect is also an area where HR Analytics can support the recruiting and selection process.

The last criterion in the formula is motivation: does the employee want to do the job? Candidates may have the right personality, the right skill set and knowledge, but may not want to do this job for a variety of reasons. Maybe they think the pay is not enough, or the work location is too far away from where they live. HR analytics can help suss out these elements as well and determine the probability of success, or at least of retention, of each candidate.

Often, a point is made that, for motivational fit, if the person isn't interested, he or she wouldn't have applied for the job. There are many who think money is the main motivation to take a new job. In other words, even if a candidate says: 'you can't pay me enough to do this', there is a point where the answer is yes, if the proposed pay doubled/tripled/ten times? But, most of the time, money is not the only motivator. Take, for instance, a fresh graduate: what motivated them? It could be that they are mostly motivated by money because they want to start earning their own instead of taking money from their parents. But they may also want to get into a role where they feel they are learning, contributing and adding value. Others may be keener on the reputation of the firm and how it reflects on them/looks on their CV ('If I got into Google, I must be good! Let me post it online and let everybody know!'). Sometimes, even if the candidate is not initially motivated, the firm can find a way to provide the motivation, by re-designing the job, adjusting the job title, allowing for more work-from-home scheduling, etc. Thus, future success depends on motivation and HR analytics can help to uncover this.

The formula uses a multiplier among these criteria to emphasise the point that each of these criteria increases someone's chance of success of the job. So, if a candidate has the right personality, it makes a big difference if they also have the right skill and knowledge. And if they have the right skill and the right personality, it makes a big difference when they also have the right motivation.

The weightage assigned to each criterion will depend on the requirements of the job. For example, a consulting executive may weigh personality and motivational fit higher than the others because, in this environment, it may be that if the candidate is really intent on a consulting career and has the right personality, they will pick up the required skills. If the firm does not expect a fresh graduate to come in and be able to consult immediately, they can place less emphasis on skill. On other jobs, for example payroll accounting, candidates are expected to apply their skills immediately the day they walk in. If so, skill becomes more important. It depends on the job and it may depend on the organisation's needs and expectations as well; will they pay a candidate to learn?

A consequence of the multiplicative nature of the formula is that, even if area is off, the candidate may still have a reasonable chance of success if they have everything else right.

8.3.3 Using Tests

Taking heed of the above-mentioned logic, it follows that HR analytics will need to measure some of these things that may seem quite abstract, for example, motivation and personality attributes. To do so, using tests is important, but it should only be part of the data used, not the only piece of data. Nevertheless, organisations that hire a lot of people, like IT firms or large manufacturing plants, are more efficient and effective at finding a way to filter candidates (see Fig. 8.5).

The testing can function as a filtering process. Typically, this is done through an assessment centre. It is basically a 'day-in-the-life' of what the job is all about. In the majority of cases the test resembles a 'worst day-in-the-life'! If the candidate comes out still feeling energised, still being motivated, it would suggest they are probably suited for the job. This type of test gives candidates a taste what it feels like to be in that job. The recruiter and HR analysts can then compare scores to ascertain which candidates can perform best as well as determine which have the highest motivation to do the job. Bear in mind that, whatever the test is used, it is not

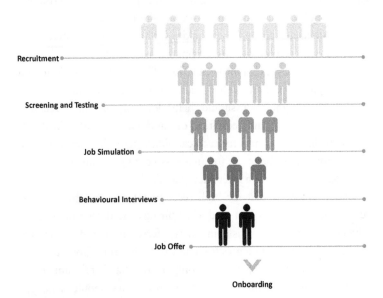

Fig. 8.5. Selection Funnel.

foolproof. No result is ever 100% accurate, as results only aim to increase the probability of a good hire. In addition, there is always the likelihood of sheer luck, or that candidates find a way to game the system.

Results of assessments normally comprise two main elements: signs and samples. Signs are measures of factors that may influence an individual's ability to perform in a role. In other words, the underlying abilities, attributes and preferences. Samples are observations and examples of an individual's ability to perform important aspects of a role. That is to say, the underlying behaviours. Typically, whether the filtering is in the form of an assessment centre or a situational judgement test, decisions are made based on a given situation which is closely related to the decisions they would have to make on the job. That is a *sample*. A *sign*, on the other hand, is a trait, a personality and attribute. Most personality tests like DISC, MBTI, etc. rely only on signs. Personality tests ask questions of the type: 'I like the smell of roses in the morning', or 'I hate a puppy licking my face'. Those are signs and not a sample because the tester did not put the puppy in front of the candidate, have it lick their face and look at how they reacted. Nonetheless, they also provide valuable input to the process of determining which candidate has the higher probability of success.

Tests help to reduce bias by taking away the human interaction. Ideally, test results can be compared to standards and norms against your target/current population. This is when the discussion on sampling we had earlier becomes relevant. If the tests are accurate enough, they should help not only in the screening, selection, filtering and recruiting of candidates but also in developing training programs for each candidate upon their arrival in the company, rather than wait for an assessment by the supervisor and/ or HR, a year or more after they joined.

Tests are best used for both recruitment and selection. To be clear, recruitment is often used when hiring candidates from outside the company. Selection is sometimes referred to as the process for selecting internal candidates for a new or higher role. Good tests are objective; there will be a norm comparative that is relevant to the job/location/age group/industry of interest. They should also support the interview process in a cost-effective way. Used correctly, tests constitute a valid selection technique. On the other hand, some of the disadvantages include the following:

- Administration time, which may be longer than interviews in some cases.

- Valid tests in some cases require a comprehensive job analysis to understand the job before the test can be designed and built.

- Cost of materials and training can sometimes be an issue.

- There can also be potential legal issues if tests are not used correctly; for instance, if used as the sole basis for hiring and selection decisions, as the test can be biased and, as mentioned before, not meant to be used by itself but as a means to support the rest of the process.

- In some cases, there are people with tests anxiety, not good at taking tests which will affect their results.

- Sometimes candidates can cheat, some because they can ask people who took the test previously, or they can get copies on the internet (this is particularly true if the tests are over-exposed), or if left alone in a room, they can ask other candidates or look at their answers.

- Tests that are not well designed, run into validity and prediction issues.

Note that the cost of an assessment centre is different than for a test. An assessment centre can cost up to a five-figure sum per person. A test is typically two to three figures. Assessment centres are best used for senior-level hires: CEO selection, heads of department and the like.

8.3.4 Assessments in the Workplace

There are a few categories of tests in the workplace, namely, Personality/Behaviours tests, Interests/Motives tests, Cognitive Abilities tests and a broad array of other types of tests.

Personality assessments aim to describe aspects of an individual's characteristics (patterns of behaviour, thoughts, feelings) that remain stable throughout the individual's lifetime, and how these are expressed at the workplace. There are a large number of valid personality tests available. Some of the more well-known include DISC, MBTI, five-factor model and the trait model. All of them have their own theoretical basis and all of them can claim to have validity, reliability and generalisability over the domain they test. A personality test aims to highlight an individual's traits (is the person an introvert/extrovert, is the candidate a detail-oriented person or a big-picture person, etc.) so they can be correlated with on-the-job performance.

Interest inventories help identify career interests and occupational themes. Motives/Values inventories assess the core goals, values, drivers and interests that determine what we desire and strive to attain. These are mostly used for career coaching. For instance, most universities with a career coaching department will have one or more of these inventories which students can take to help them understand what career/job they should want to do.

Cognitive ability tests assess an individual's mental abilities or processes to carry out simple/complex tasks linked to how we learn, remember and solve problems. This is a traditional choice of many organisations: Is this person smart? Can they reason? Can they analyse, etc?

There are a host of other assessment tests available. Many of them are skills tests to assess basic skills such as customer handling, typing, manual skills, IT applications, etc. Included in this category are also Situational Judgement Tests for many different types of career battery assessment. For example, for assessing nurses, it is possible to use a nursing career battery, a team-career battery, professional-career battery, etc., all related to expectations for success in that profession. These are often also normed and validated globally.

SUMMARY

In this chapter we covered the application of data and analytics in recruitment, along with the basics of sampling methods. The key message is that HR analytics can be of help in recruiting by helping the hiring manager and the recruiting function to hire the best possible pool of candidates based on data; not gut feel or 'intuition'. However, we also discussed that no single tool is the BEST predictor: It is therefore important to use a holistic approach involving more than one test/tool to arrive at more robust recruiting decisions.

One closing thought for this chapter is the idea that HR analytics can help determine how recruiting metrics could be a predictor or antecedent for business performance. For instance, there is some evidence to support the idea that boards and companies that are more diverse (in terms of employee profile) outperform those that are homogeneous. By finding how this relationship works in the company (see the discussion at the end of Chapter 1), HR analytics can help add value to the company by helping to determine the optimum level of diversity.

QUESTIONS

1. Will an Artificial Intelligence–based system be able to recruit more accurately than managers? What are the potential advantages and risks of automated recruiting?

2. How to ensure machine learning algorithms do not learn the same mistakes and biases that currently affect the recruiting process?

3. How would you measure the efficiency and effectiveness of new methods of recruiting vs the traditional methods?

9

COMPENSATION AND BENEFITS

In this chapter we will look into the application of conjoint analysis and MANOVA as analytic tools to look into compensation and benefits plan design.

When organisations make a reward plan decision, it often aims to do three things: One is to ensure the employees perceive the new or revised plan well. Normally these perceptions are analysed and communicated in the form of market benchmarking: 'is the plan competitive?' The second thing organisations are concerned with when making rewards decision is the cost. While on the one hand it is important that employees perceive that the reward plans are tailored to their needs and in line with what the market offers, on the other hand, it must be affordable. The third area is critical: are rewards tied to the strategy of the organisation? For example, if an organisation pays more in fixed pay, it could be that a large number of employees like this approach. However, that may not be tied to the desired strategic outcome if the company aspires to be a performance-based organisation.

Very often, organisations do not know exactly how much they spend on each reward plan because they may not have quantified the items, benefits or programs, even if they can tell what the overall benefits cost or bonus cost is. At the same time, employees seldom know the cost of benefit plans. And while they may, individually, know their own perception of the rewards program, employers generally have a limited view of these perceptions, and probably refer to an engagement survey that asks: 'Are you paid fairly for the work you do in this organisation?'

HR analytics can help tackle these questions. We have chosen to focus on benefits in this chapter, which seldom get enough attention.

9.1 HR ANALYTICS AND BENEFITS

Benefits are, by their nature, perceived by most HR functions as less strategic, almost as an afterthought. In the 'attraction/ retention/motivation' way of thinking of many HR departments, benefits at best play some role in retention. However, HR analytics can help to look at benefits in a way that would allow organisations to get a better sense of how they can be used for attraction and retention. In particular, benefits share an interesting characteristic in that the value of the benefit is often not related to the perceived value of the benefit. That means, the benefit may cost the company a significant amount of money and yet employees assign it little or no value. Or vice versa, the benefit may not cost the company much, but to the employees the perceived value is very high. Features that motivate one group of employees may be completely irrelevant to a different group. Note that the perceived value of a benefit depends on what each individual thinks the benefit is worth; it is not a single, uniform value across all employees. We can use HR analytics to identify the mismatch between what the company is spending on benefits and what employees truly value.

For example, assume that an organisation's head of compensation believes that one way to reduce turnover is to introduce a generous health insurance plan. Specifically, a health insurance plan that has a very good childbirth benefit so that, if a female employee giving birth needs to have a C-section, the coverage is substantial. To a 30–35-year-old female who has been married a few years and is beginning to contemplate having children, then this plan would have great value. But to a young male employee, recently graduated and not yet married, this plan would not be of much value. The plan may, as the head of compensation expects, help to lower turnover in the company, but it would only impact a limited segment of the population: females in childbearing years, and males that have spouses in childbearing years. Similarly, the same head of compensation may be thinking of introducing a pension plan to further aid in staff retention, but it may well be that only employees above 50 years of age would consider this a valuable benefit, while most millennials in the company would not assign any worth to it as, in their minds, the probability of retiring from the company, 20 years or more into the future, is practically zero. Thus, the perceived value differs according to each person, which has led companies to create flexible benefit plans. Interests may not only vary by life stage, but also by location, job category and other groupings that are less obvious.

But what combination of benefits would yield the best results under a flexible plan? The traditional way in which many companies approach this problem is to work through an insurance broker and look at market data: 'Companies in your industry/of your size do this and this; You should do slightly better'. However, this approach does not consider the preferences of the companies' employees. HR analytics can help the head of compensation to determine what the degree of preference for each proposed benefit is, and by which group of employees. One way to approach this as a business problem is to think of how do benefits compare to other rewards programs that the company could be implementing, or improving, with the same amount of money. If the head of compensation in our example has an extra 5% of total people cost as a budget that he could spend to improve retention, would it be better to hire 5% more people, pay everyone 5% more, add 5% to the target bonus of all staff, provide 5% better benefits, or some combination? How would our head of compensation know which is the best thing to do? What HR analytics can help do is to create an optimal combination of perceived value vs actual value for each benefit, by employee groups/demographics. If one size does not fit all, how can the head of compensation come to understand which benefit plan features offer the optimal combination of value to employees and cost-savings for the firm? How best to identify the unique combination of rewards (health benefits, compensation, leave, etc.) – considering the plan elements that have low cost but high-perceived value – that can better engage and retain employees?

Conjoint analysis is an excellent tool to help answer this type of question. However, it's important to understand that conjoint analysis is different than surveys. A survey provides answers such as: '57% of employees want to do this and 42% wants to do that', maybe even by demographics, and some sort of ranking. Conjoint analysis, on the other hand, combines analytics with real staff scenarios and expectations.

9.2 CONJOINT ANALYSIS

Conjoint analysis is a useful approach to measure the value that individuals place on features of a product or service. It does this by combining real-life scenarios and statistical techniques with the modelling of actual decisions. To implement this approach in the rewards arena, companies can ask employees to evaluate a series of factors such as wages, health benefits, flexible schedule, retirement benefits, wellness programs, gym membership discounts, dental allowance, phone allowance, childcare benefits, study leave, paid time off, etc.

Fig. 9.1 shows an example of possible factors to consider in a conjoint analysis.

The objective is to understand what employees consider the most important elements of benefits, by individual, group or segment. A key outcome is to determine the relative importance of these benefits, as they impact attraction, retention and performance levels, as well as to identify which elements can be cut back or minimised in building benefit programs.

9.2.1 Methods of Conjoint Analyses

There are a variety of ways in which conjoint analysis can be carried out. In the following sections we highlight a few of the main approaches used (See Fig. 9.1 for examples of the tools used for these approaches):

Learning	On-the job training	Leadership/management development programmes	On-the job training	My current total rewards package is preferable
Career Advancement	Exposure to opportunities/projects outside of your current department/business unit – may include overseas assignments	Fast tracking career progression to executive or senior management levels	Promotion within current business unit/function	
Remuneration	Base salary targeting the top end of the market and retention bonus	Base salary targeting the upper end of the market	Base salary targeting the upper end of the market	
Benefits	Employer contributes 100% of total retirement fund contribution plus highest level of medical cover	0% employer contribution to retirement fund plus basic medical cover	Employer contributes 100% of total retirement fund contribution plus highest level of medical cover	
Work–Life Balance	Flexible work hours	Flexible work hours	Flexible work hours	
Performance and Recognition	Short-term incentives linked to your performance plus Stock options or shares	Short-term incentives linked to your performance plus Stock options or shares	Short-term incentive linked to your performance	

Fig. 9.1. Possible Factors to Include in a Conjoint Analysis of Total Rewards.

9.2.1.1. Two-item tradeoff analysis

- In this approach, the survey tool presents a series of item-by-item (two items at a time) tradeoff tables for respondents to rank their preference for the items.

- For example, if there are three benefits, the table would have nine cells and the respondents would rank their tradeoff preferences from 1 to 9.

- The two-item-at-a-time approach makes few cognitive demands of the respondent and is simple to follow, but it is tedious and limited in the number of items that can be analysed.

- There are limits to this approach. For example, if there are 11 benefits to compare, you will have 55 comparisons. Respondents may find it cumbersome to compare so many items, may not be able to compare them properly as some may begin to look alike, and may get tired of answering these questions after some time.

9.2.1.2. Self-explicated conjoint analysis

- This approach uses a tool that shows all elements of a remuneration package and asks the respondent to allocate 100 points across these elements in a way that reflects the importance placed on each element.

- For example, four remuneration packages may be shown, ranked by most to least favourable, based on a person's allocation.

- Employees confirm their initial allocation was correct by agreeing to the ranking or go back and adjust their allocation. This process is repeated until the employee agrees with the rankings.

- In this approach, employees explicitly provide the quantification of importance and the size of relative rankings with their allocation decisions. That is to say, not just the ranking of the benefits, but the relative importance among them.

9.2.1.3. Maximum difference conjoint analysis

- Employees are shown several unique combinations of benefits package elements. For each set of elements, they are asked which element is the least important and which is the most important to them.

- Statistical modelling is used to infer the quantification of the absolute and relative importance of each element of the remuneration package.

- Useful for examining the relative importance of general elements (e.g. the importance of health care coverage vs dental coverage vs retirement plan).

- Not recommended for determining the relative importance of specific levels of the benefit plan elements (e.g. full dental coverage vs 50% dental coverage vs 20% 15 days of paid childcare leave vs 18 days of paid childcare leave). In other words, this approach works best to determine the relative position of most and least preferred benefits but may not be able to assign an accurate relative value for those not often identified as most or least preferred.

9.2.1.4. Adaptive conjoint analysis

- Adaptive conjoint analysis varies the choice sets presented to respondents based on their preference.

- The adaptation targets the employee's most preferred features, making the conjoint exercise more efficient.

- Often more engaging to the survey-taker and shortens the survey length without significantly diminishing the power of the conjoint analysis.

A word of caution when constructing conjoint analysis tools: It is important that respondents clearly understand the difference among the choices presented to that their choices are valid. For instance, it would not be useful to ask a respondent to express a preference receiving one restricted stock unit or a number of stock options, if they do not know the difference among these; they must be explained as needed. However, this example highlights the value of a conjoint analysis to uncover perceived versus actual value: At which point would employees prefer stock options over restricted shares? The survey can ask for responses to items such as: 'two options better than one share', 'three options better than one share', 'four options better than one share', to figure at what point people change their preference. If, for instance, the real value is that one restricted share is worth four stock options, and people respond that they are willing to trade one share for three options, the company could gain in the perceived value of the shares program at a lower cost (note that the organisation could also choose to deliver a higher perceived value at the same cost).

9.2.1.5. Segment conjoint results to find trends in the data[1]

The HR analyst should expect that different demographic groups will have different preferences when it comes to how they would like their compensation to be delivered. For instance, late-career employees may have a lower risk profile than junior employees and thus place a higher value on restricted stock or on cash than on share options. Demographic analysis is also likely to show that the value placed on different alternatives will vary among business units or geographies, which may help to design more aligned strategies and debunk – through actual data – the 'one size fits all' strategy.

Prior employee experience may also influence the value they assign to each alternative. Those employees who have enjoyed share price gains from previous share option plans (think Apple, Google, Amazon or Microsoft in the early days) may be more likely to place a higher value on them than those who saw their share plans come to naught during flat or declining markets. Conjoint analysis may help to understand what are the patterns in the data and from there the HR analyst can build hypotheses: Could it be that people who have been in the company longer prefer stock options, and the people who have been in the company less time prefer share grants?

---

[1]With thanks to Sidharth Mehta, Mercer, for his valuable contribution to this section.

Fig. 9.2. Examples of Conjoint Surveys.

Less easy to see via demographic segmentation analysis, but not less important, is the impact that perceived career opportunities may have on value preferences. It may well be that, those employees planning to stay with the company long enough to vest in their awards, will have a higher perceived value than those that do not expect to stay in the company that long. Conjoint analysis may give insights into the tipping point for vesting; long enough to encourage retention, but not so long as to have no meaningful perceived value.

The flip side of such an analysis could be an additional hypothesis related to the probability that people will stay in the company according to their benefits preferences. Looking at patterns of preferences between stock options vs performance shares, and similar plans, may lead to interesting results. For instance, if there is a pattern in the data that say most people with less than five years in the company want short-term gains, but those with more than five years want long-term gains, it may be possible to hypothesise that people with longer tenure tend to not want to leave, whereas the people who do not intend to stay place less value on long-term benefits.

Fig. 9.3 shows possible results of the attributes shown in Fig. 9.1.

Attribute	Level	Level Description	Utility	Relative Importance of Attribute	Ranking
Learning	3	On-the-job training	-153.17	9.1%	5
	2	MBA tuition reimbursement	9.76		
	1	Leadership development programmes	143.41		
Career Advancement	3	Promotion within current department	-132.94	10.3%	4
	2	Exposure to opportunities outside of your current department and country	203.03		
	1	Fast-tracking career progression to senior management levels	-70.08		
Remuneration	3	Base salary targeting at 50th percentile of the market	-349.94	17.0%	3
	2	Base salary targeting at 75th percentile of the market	147.46		
	1	Base salary targeting the top end of the market and retention bonus	202.48		
Benefits	3	0% employer contribution to retirement fund plus basic medical cover	-679.13	35.2%	1
	2	Employer contributes 50% of total retirement fund contribution plus moderate level of medical cover	210.18		
	1	Employer contributes 100% of total retirement fund contribution plus highest level of medical cover	468.94		
Work–Life Balance	3	Flexible work hours	171.32	8.4%	6
	2	Work from home	-101.70		
	1	Reduced work load	-69.61		
Performance and Recognition	3	On the spot awards e.g. gift vouchers, verbal recognition	-355.00	20.0%	2
	2	Short-term incentive linked to your performance	58.28		
	1	Short-term incentives linked to your performance (plus stock options or shares)	296.71		

Fig. 9.3. Possible Results of the Conjoint Analysis of Total Rewards.

9.2.1.5.1. Multivariate Analysis of Variance (MANOVA). Multivariate Analysis of Variance (MANOVA) is similar to ANOVA, except that there is more than one variable (or factors) involved. This is used in analysis where more than one factor affects the dependent variable. That is to say, ANOVA checks for the differences between the means of two samples from the same population, whereas MANOVA checks for differences between multiple samples of the same population. In fact, MANOVA can be thought of as a generalisation of ANOVA.

MANOVA looks at the interactions among and between the dependent and independent variables. When the various factors affecting the dependent variable, including all their combinations at different levels, are tested, we call this 'factorial experiments'.

MANOVA should be used when the data include continuous response variables that are correlated. In addition to multiple responses, MANOVA is useful where there are multiple factors, covariates and interactions in the model (see Fig. 9.2). For example, think of a data set that includes employee information related to salary and salary grade, and also information on level of education and intent to leave. These data are likely to be correlated to each other (level of education to salary grade, salary grade to salary, salary to intent to leave, etc.). However, it could be that, when using ANOVA to test each of these separately, results are not statistically significant (pay alone does not explain intent to leave, for instance). But when looking at these together using MANOVA, the results may show that those individuals with high educational level, low pay and in a high salary grade may have a higher score on intent to leave. The combination of factors in the analysis may lead to a better understanding of the trends (Fig. 9.4).

9.3 THINKING ANALYTICALLY ABOUT COMPENSATION

HR analytics can be of much use to look into the organisation's compensation and practices. Using the available data from the HRIS system, and adding additional data such as engagement scores, there are many hypotheses, insights and stories that can be derived.

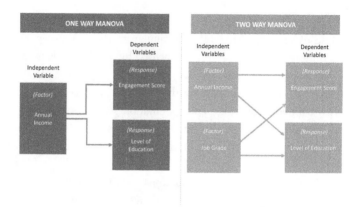

Fig. 9.4. Illustration of MANOVA.

Following are some examples to illustrate how HR analytics could be used in compensation with the objective of improving the performance of the organisation. Note that MANOVA can be used in several of these examples.

- Pay effectiveness: Are the company's incentive systems yielding the right results? It is often difficult to determine if pay causes results, or results cause pay. To address this issue, it is possible to analyse over time if changes in the compensation policies translate into changes in performance. Often the data will have other variables that can cause 'noise', but supplemented with qualitative data, it is possible to determine if the programs are working. Another way to address this is to have pilot programs, where it is easier to see how changes in pay schemes can drive desired behaviours and outcomes. This is a superior alternative to matching the organisation's pay scheme to the market or to competitors and 'wishing for the best under the assumption that this is how it is done.'

- Team vs Individual incentives: Pilot programs can help here as well. Would a 100% team incentive drive better outcome than a mix of team vs individual or than a 100% individual-based incentive? Many times, the assumptions made (e.g. 'a mix of individual and team is the best way to go') are not based on analysis. Yet, to reiterate, ideally, all assumptions should be tested in the context of the characteristics and culture of each organisation.

- Merit Pay differentials: How much more should an above average performer receive as a percentage of merit increase, compared to an average performance? How about an outstanding performer in comparison to an above average performer? This question can be turned on its head to be more useful in an analytical context: How much more merit pay will motivate an average performer to increase his level of performance to above average? And how much more for an above average performer to increase to an outstanding level of performance? When the question is asked this way, we will look for ways to improve performance; when asked the first way, we are looking for ways to reward performance. Not the same outcome!

- Target setting: When determining outstanding or threshold levels of performance, how high or low should these be set? One approach that can be used is to look at historical data and pick the right percentile (say 70% achievement for threshold, and 20% achievement for outstanding). Conversely, this can also be achieved by picking standard deviations (say 2-sigma below average historical performance for threshold and 3-sigma for outstanding).

- Pay Mix: Should pay mix be set according to the market data? Or is there a better amount for pay mix that can drive better performance? As mentioned, this is another hypothesis that can be tested with historical data (if the organisation has enough data points), or by running pilots. In one example, one of the authors created a four-tiered pilot for salespeople in a fast-moving consumer goods company in Latin America. With 10 sales territories which were matched by size and sales patterns, two were control territories and the other eight had two of each under the following conditions of pay mix: 80/20, 70/30, 60/40 and 50/50. Statistically the results showed that the 60/40 model yielded the best results after one year, and the entire company shifted to this pay mix (it was originally 40/60). Sales and employee retention both increased.

- Diversity: How many males and females are there in the organisation? Are they paid equivalently? Are they promoted equally? Do the numbers vary by length of service? Are there pockets of employees (e.g. engineers, support staff, accountants) that skew the numbers? Perhaps there are more females in the lower grades than in the higher grades? Are there too many (or too few) females in certain jobs/functions/levels/locations?

The point we make in this section is that the use of HR analytics can help to create insights which can be used to communicate to senior management about ways to modify the pay schemes to better drive business results.

SUMMARY

In this chapter we have covered how to use analytical tools (we focused on conjoint analysis and MANOVA) to help organisations achieve better performance and retention through pay and benefits.

QUESTIONS

1. Which approach would you propose to use to test each of the points mentioned in Section 9.3? Note that there is already an example provided under the 'Pay Mix' bullet point.

2. Specifically, how would you test to determine if there is pay discrimination between males and females in the company?

3. In which other area of HR do you think that Conjoint Analysis and MANOVA can be useful tools for analysis?

4. If from prior analysis it has been found that the company's R&D staff are motivated by different things than the salespeople, would you want to put in place the same benefit plans for both of them, or instead implement different plans?

5. How long do you think pay data collected today will stay valid?

CASELET: USING CONJOINT ANALYSIS TO CREATE REWARDS PROGRAMS[2]

This global hospitality group was at risk of losing future revenue because its workforce was not customer-centric enough to retain high-value customers, even as the organisation was in the midst of a revamp and re-branding to become more service-focused.

Among other areas, the HR analytics team went to work to optimising the reward program to drive the desired customer-centric culture. The analysis included a review of the current benefits portfolio (e.g. health, on-site facilities, allowances, bonuses, pensions).

To collect data, the HR analytics team used a data-driven method called TRiO, which aims to optimise the investments in rewards programs by assessing cost vs preference choices by employees. TRiO involves conjoint analysis surveys for employees and a dashboard for project stakeholders to establish a quantitative view of how employees perceive value.

The dashboard plots plan cost on the horizontal axis and the perception of rewards – via the conjoint survey responses – on the vertical axis. Through this tool, what the organisation was trying to do is to either choose plans with a positive perception keeping cost similar or to decrease the cost and keep plan perceptions similar. The result is a curve, a sort of 'efficient frontier' of the total reward investment (see Fig. 9.5 below). Within the area inside the curve, the company is either saving costs, or increasing plan perception, or doing both.

Via this analysis, which also included other factors such as strategic alignment, risk and competitiveness, the team was able to identify the combinations of reward elements yielding the maximum effectiveness at various levels of cost. The analysis also yielded a series of insights which included the attribution of high value to career development and annual leave.

The end result was that the organisational change was supported by multiple solutions. In the case of rewards, the analysis led to action planning on engagement improvement with each division

---

[2]With thanks to Samir Bedi for his valuable contributions to this section.

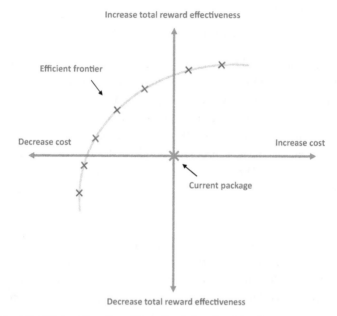

Fig. 9.5. Efficient Frontier of Benefits Using Conjoint Analysis.

(casino, hotels, F&B, etc.). The company even used these results to negotiate with the union on certain benefits and terms.

The results proved to be sustainable and provided greater alignment to the new customer-centred strategies.

Below we provide more details on the survey and the results.

Firstly, it is important to codify the demographics: Age, gender, department, level in the organisation, tenure, etc.

Next, are the rewards plans being tested; in this example, the company included 12 different rewards components. For each one of these elements, the company had a cost associated to it. This is the most critical part of the analysis: to determine what are the rewards elements the organisation wanted to test. The main issue is to only include elements that they were willing to change, as well as the minimum and maximum they were willing to go with each plan along with the current offer.

This survey would then show each participating employee a series of choices related to the 12 rewards programs chosen. The choices were combined into a 'basket of goods'. For example, would the employee prefer a salary increase of 6.5% no wellness program? Or a salary increase of 5% coupled with the availability of healthy snacks at work with a 75% discount? Would the employee prefer a company-provided mobile phone with no reimbursement? Or to bring their own device with a company reimbursement plan?

The fundamental idea behind this approach is that both options in each case cost the company the same amount. Employees are asked questions on each of the 12 items up to 12 times. If, for instance, salary increase is coming up as a preferred option, after a few iterations of the survey the company kept salary increase fixed and asked questions on other areas. So, we're trying to get a preference of those benefit items. Similarly, if a specific plan was showing no preference, it would be eliminated from future iterations and new elements would be included.

After the team collected all the data inputs, they went on to test the benefits and the quantum of those benefits. The benefits package costs the company $26 million. The objective was to create either a higher value package at the same or lower cost, or to lower the plan costs at either the same or higher perceived value. The dashboard allowed for analysing possible changes to the plans: For example, bonus came out as the highest preference and life insurance as second. What if bonus went to 40% instead the score it received of 60%; would it remain number one?

It is important to note how strategic alignment was included in the analysis. For the 12 items that were tested in this case, there was a back-end scoring of their alignment to the business strategy. In other words, the bonus plan and long-term plan were given higher scores. Thus, any time someone chose a lower bonus or a lower long-term incentive, the strategic alignment score would fall because the organisation wanted to drive a performance-based strategy. The ideal situation is to have perception increasing, alignment increasing and cost decreasing. However, the efficient frontier only considers cost and perceived value, not strategic alignment; alignment needs to be tested point by point.

By doing this analysis, the organisation ended up with two alternative designs: One alternative would keep cost the same at $26 million but the perceived value had gone up by more than 8% and the alignment to the business strategy had gone up by 51%. That meant that employees perceived this group of benefit programs to be better than the current plan and the company benefitted by having this design be more aligned to the new customer-centric strategy. The second alternative yielded a design where the cost has gone up by $9 million, the perceived value was the same and the alignment had decreased by more than 20%. The company opted to not go with this alternative because, even though it was going to cost less, it was not as aligned to the change in business strategy. In the past, the organisation was only able to rely on only market benchmarks. They would say, for example: 'our competitors are offering five years' life insurance, we are only offering three years, therefore we need to increase to offer five years' worth'. The HR analytics team was able to come up with this model to evaluate reward plans trade-offs in totality: 'Our dental benefits are not so competitive, but we offer better parental leave and that has a higher preference'.

When presenting the proposed design to senior management, the team had to address a few additional questions: What if the bonus was increased by another 5%? What if the life insurance program was increased to five times of salary from three times of salary? The dashboard allowed the team to return to the efficient frontier to respond: 'Doing that could increase perceived value, and will increase/maintain alignment, but will cost $5 million more'.

A few refinements considered for the next years include insights derived from analysing the data by demographics to tailoring programs for specific groups. For example, the organisation noticed that the age of individuals retiring from the company has been increasing every year. In the past, employees would retire at an average age of around 55 years but lately, that number has increased to between 60 and 65 years. This trend translates into higher expenditure as these employees are more costly and also prevent career growth opportunities for other employees. The company is using the conjoint analysis model to determine what it can offer employees over 55 years of age to change to a more flexible kind of role rather than full-time kind of role, and still be paid enough while contributing in terms of knowledge. They are going after this alternative carefully since, as is the case in any employee survey (and the conjoint survey qualifies as such), the company is concerned of raising high expectations prematurely.

10

CAREER PLANNING

This chapter looks at career planning and mobility, using decision trees as our analytics tool. At the end of the chapter we will walk through a case example using analytics for career pathing.

One way to think of career planning is as a decision tree that has nodes and probabilities. This is a slightly different way to look at things, in the sense that we are not here looking at the organisational patterns as was the case with compensation in the previous chapter. When we look at career planning, the unit of analysis is more the individual. As an HR professional, the key question we are addressing is to have a conversation with employees about how to decide their own career and which path they can follow to get there. An advantage of this approach, from an HR functional standpoint, is that it helps to ensure that there are enough people being prepared for succession in our talent and workforce planning. Or that, if there are not enough successors being prepared, it can help decide whether it is best to buy talent, instead of building talent.

The more the organisations believe the answer is building talent, the more it should know what is the probability that by following specific career paths, employees will stay and will be prepared for future roles. Career plans, therefore, need to come together with competency models, talent development and training. In the following sections we delve into applying HR analytics to this problem of how to ensure there are enough staff being prepared to build the organisation's future talent.

10.1 USING ANALYTICS TO DETERMINE MOBILITY POSSIBILITIES

Career paths can be thought of as models or prototypes characterising the career sequences of an individual, or of a common group of individuals. Career sequences, in turn, depict the succession of occupational jobs within an individual or similar group of individuals' work history.

There are several types of career mobility possibilities; for example:

- Movements across organisations within occupations

- Movements across occupations within organisations

- Movements across both occupations and organisations

- Movements across countries, etc.

Analytics can be very helpful in determining mobility options. It is particularly useful to weigh variables such as assignment duration, purpose, status (temporary or permanent) and potential dependencies. Decision tree analysis can aid in determining which candidates are most suited to each assignment. Let us look at that last sentence in more detail. A career path basically means that every time an employee gets promoted, that promotion leads them in a certain direction for the rest of their career, and often precludes them (unless they return to an earlier stage) to follow some other direction for the rest of their career. In short, taking a path is akin to a decision node in a decision tree. And each decision is tied to a probability that this particular path chosen will lead to other career moves that eventually will allow the employee to reach their ultimate career goal.

There are many types of career paths. The most common path starts from individual contributor roles in an area of speciality, through supervisory and managerial roles, to an eventual role in senior management. There are also technical career paths, in which employees progress through an increasingly more complex set of issues addressed in a specific technical field. There can be career paths that start technical and then become managerial. Or a permeable career path, which means employees can have a stint in a managerial role to then come back to the technical path. Often employees build their own career path: 'I want to try this area in this company because I want to learn this skill, then I want to progress to that company so I can capitalise on the expertise I have gained'. In any case, whether the decision was made by the company or the employee, it changes the probability that they will achieve their career objective.

Where to start the planning is an interesting discussion. Employees, and sometimes HR departments, start with current role in mind, and try to project forward. In other words, when career planning starts with the current job, it is likely they can only see the next job and maybe some vague sense about the possibility of another role, or industry, in the future. Career planning is best started from the opposite end, say in 20 years' time. For instance, let us assume that the company (or the individual, for that matter) would like to see this employee become the Global HR Head. This change of perspective sets a different way to think about career paths: To reach that job, what should be the job before that, and then the job before that. In other words: to be the Global Head of HR, there should be a role where the person learns about working in foreign country; maybe another role where they learn resource allocation and finance; maybe even a role where they learn more about the business, or sales, or operations. This path to be the Global Head of HR involves having all of these experiences along the way. The alternative is a 'straight' path that goes from HR analyst to HR executive, to HR supervisor, to HR manager, to HR director, to HR VP to HR head. And yet, the probability of reaching that Global HR Head role by following the straight path is different (probably lower) than the probability reaching the top HR job via finance, operations, sales, etc. That is to say, although there are different career paths to get to the end, the probability of getting there differs according to the path chosen.

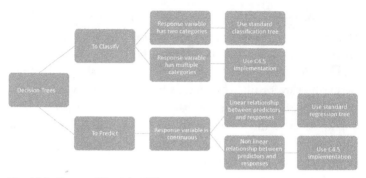

Fig. 10.1. Types of Decision Trees.

10.2 DECISION TREES

A decision tree is a graphical model to structure a decision problem involving uncertainty. Decision trees are most useful when the response variable is numeric or continuous. In other words, the predicted outcome of a set of mutually exclusive decisions. In this sense, decision trees are best for prediction, as opposed to classification, problems. There are also classification trees, which separate the data set into classes belonging to the response variable (usually Yes or No [1 or 0]). Classification trees are used when the response is categorical in nature. Fig. 10.1 shows various types of decision trees. Please note that C4.5 is a type of decision tree used for classification, often used in machine learning.

10.2.1 Example of a Decision Tree

As described, decision trees model sequences of decisions and outcomes over time. Many problems involve making a choice between a small set of decisions with uncertain consequences. When formulating a decision problem, these involve:

- The decision alternatives.

- The uncertain events that may occur after a decision is made, along with their possible outcomes ('states of nature') and defined so that only one of them will occur.

- The consequences associated with each decision and outcome, usually expressed as payoffs. These are sometimes summarised in payoff tables (rows correspond to decisions and columns to events).

The various parts of a decision tree are as follows:

- Nodes: Points in time at which events take place

- Decision Nodes: Nodes in which a decision takes place by choosing among alternatives (represent features/attributes)

- Event Nodes: Nodes in which an event occurs that are not controlled by the decision-maker

- Branches: These are the possible outcomes associated with decisions and events

The decision-maker first selects a decision alternative, after which one of the outcomes of the uncertain event occurs, resulting in the payoff.

Fig. 10.2 illustrates a typical decision tree. This company is considering developing one of two types of products (Product A and Product X). The company does not have the capability and capacity to do both, so must choose one or the other, or it can choose to do neither. Which one should they focus on? If it develops Product A, it

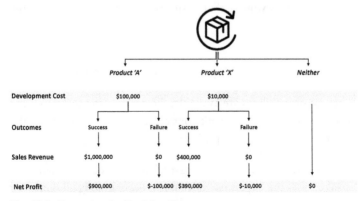

Fig. 10.2. Example of a Decision Tree.

will cost \$100,000, whereas development of Product X will cost \$10,000. Note that, in this example, doing nothing costs nothing and has no future revenue either. If Product X succeeds in the market, the company stands to earn \$400,000 minus what it invested in it. If it does not succeed, the company loses what it invested. If it decides to do Product A, and it fails, the company will have spent \$100,000; if it succeeds, it earns \$1,000,000, of which they keep \$900,000 of profit. However, is this decision tree enough for the company to decide which path to follow? Let's assume that the decision was instead how much to bet on a series of coin flips, where on the first toss you determine the size of the bet (If heads you bet \$100,000 and if tails the bet is \$10,000). Then you flip a second time: if heads you win and if tails you lose. Would you take the bet? In the first case, the expected value (EV) would be \$450,000 (50% of winning \$1,000,000, minus the \$100,000 you put in). In the second case, the EV would be \$195,000 (50% of winning \$400,000, minus the \$10,000 you put in). In either case you should say 'yes' as the EV is positive (with the first case being even better). Knowing the probability of each toss helps determine your willingness to bet. Thus, what the company needs is to find out what is the probability of success and of failure in each case, and then weigh these.

Career decisions can be seen to follow a similar logic. At each decision point the employee must choose which the better bet is: should they stay in the company and take a lateral transfer to sales, or take the search firm's call about that opportunity for a bigger HR role in another industry? Knowing the probabilities of success by following either path would help in making the decision.

10.2.2 Decision Strategies without Outcome Probabilities

When no probabilities are available, the decision tree technique can be used to assess several alternative strategies to maximise the objective (e.g. payoffs are profits):

- Aggressive (Optimistic) Strategy: Choose the decision that maximises the largest payoff that can occur among all outcomes for each decision (maximax strategy)

- Conservative (Pessimistic) Strategy: Choose the decision that maximises the smallest payoff that can occur among all outcomes for each decision (maximin strategy)

- Opportunity Loss Strategy: Choose the decision that minimises the maximum opportunity loss among all outcomes for each decision (minimax regret)

Note: You can also seek to minimise the objective (e.g. reduce cost) by applying the inverse approach in each case.

10.2.3 Decision Strategies with Outcome Probabilities

In situations where there is at least some assessment for each of the outcome probabilities, either through some method of forecasting or reliance on expert opinions, we can choose the best decision based on the EV.

The simplest case is to assume that each outcome is equally likely to occur; the probability of each outcome is $1/N$, where N is the number of possible outcomes. This is called the average payoff strategy. However, this is an approach that must be used with care, as illustrated in the example of the products.

Let's illustrate this with a simple example: A food stall at the local food court sells buns stuffed with chicken for lunch. These are ordered fresh every day in batches of 100 (the supplier only sells in packages of 100 buns each) and any unsold ones at the end of the day are given to a local charity for consumption that evening, as they cannot be stored overnight. Each bun has a cost of $0.50 and they sell for $1 each. The owner has kept a record over the last 12 months which shows that the most buns he ever sold in one day was 500 and the smallest amount he ever sold was 200. Judging from his records, he knows that 25% of the days he sells 200 buns, on 50% of the days he sells 300 buns, on 20% of the days he sells 400 buns and on 5% of the days he sells 500 buns.

Putting supply and demand together, on the days he orders 200 buns, he is guaranteed to make $100, as there is a 100% chance that demand will be a minimum of 200. On the other hand, if he orders 500 buns, on 25% of the days (when demand is 200) he

Demand →	200	300	400	500	EV
Supply					
200	$100	$100	$100	$100	$100
300	$50	$150	$150	$150	$130
400	$0	$100	$200	$200	$100
500	($50)	$50	$150	$250	$55

Fig. 10.3. Supply/Demand Combinations and Possible Payoffs.

will lose $50, but on the 5% of days where demand hits 500, he will make $250! (Fig. 10.3 illustrates possible supply/demand combinations and the payoff in each case.) How many should he order?

If the owner did not know his probabilities, he could use an aggressive (optimistic) strategy and may be tempted to order 500 each day, hoping for the $250 payoff. Or he could follow a conservative strategy and always order 200, as this strategy has a no-risk level of 'guaranteed' profits. If he follows an opportunity loss strategy, he would stay away from ordering 500, as there is a chance that he would lose $50 on some days. But because he knows his probabilities, the best approach for him is to order 300, which has a higher EV. Note that we could have done this entire example using opportunity cost instead of profits. If we had used the opportunity cost, when the owner buys 200 and could have sold 300, the opportunity cost is $50 (that is, the loss of the additional profit he could have made had he bought 300 instead of 200 on that day). If he could have sold 400, the opportunity cost is $100. If he could have sold 500, the opportunity cost is $150. If he had bought 300 but only sold 200, there is no opportunity cost. If he had followed this logic, would he have made the same decision with and without knowing the probabilities?

10.3 CAREER PATHS USING DECISION TREES

This logic of using decision trees in making decisions applies equally to buns and to careers. If the probabilities of a given path leading to a certain outcome are unknown, then individuals – and HR departments – will use either an optimistic, a pessimistic or an opportunity loss strategy. A lateral move offer will not be desirable under an optimistic strategy, will seem appropriate under an opportunity loss strategy and could even be appealing under a pessimistic strategy. However, if the possibilities are available, choices on career mobility are easier to make.

How do you quantify 'probability of success' in the case of careers? If HR could keep track of the career path that each previous Global Head of HR followed, how long did each of them take to get there, and had they have had data for the last 50 Global Heads of HR, they could quantify that probability. However, it is unlikely that HR would be able to have a true assessment of probabilities. But they can make reasonable assumptions on the probabilities. A good way to approach this problem is to look prospectively by starting at the target job. For instance, let us work on an example where the company was looking to groom succession candidates to be the CEO. What possible internal jobs could an executive have had, prior to becoming the CEO? They could have been the Chief Marketing Officer (CMO), Chief Technology Officer (CTO), Chief Operating Officer (COO), Chief Financial Officer (CFO), Chief HR Officer (CHRO), Head of International Markets, Head of Domestic Market or any other job that currently reports to the CEO. HR can then work with the data at hand, and their expertise, on determining the probability of becoming the CEO if the executive is promoted from any of these jobs (assuming all other things equal). This assessment could yield results such as: CMO – 10% probability; CTO – 15%; CFO – 25%; CHRO – 3%; Head of International – 15%; Head of Domestic Market – 20%. These data may not be accurate, but they are likely directionally correct. The assessment of probabilities for each individual could be further refined by adding assessment results, past track records, previous jobs held, etc.

The next step is to continue down the decision tree branches assigning probabilities. In our example, the estimated probability of becoming the CEO from the CFO role is 25%. We can also estimate the probability of becoming the CFO if you had any of the following jobs: Head of Internal Audit – 5%; Controller – 25%; Treasurer – 15%; CTO – 10%; CHRO – 5%; Head of

International Markets – 15%; Head of Domestic Market – 20%. The same can be done for each level. If HR were to advise an executive one level below this one – for instance, the Head of Asia – about the career path to follow to fulfil their aspiration to one day be the CEO, they could advise them to aim to be promoted to Head of International or to take a lateral move to be Head of Domestic Markets, and from there either CFO or CEO directly. For each of these, there would be a probability about how each step gets this executive closer to being the CEO. From the point of view of the Head of Asia, the promotion is appealing, but has a 15% chance of later becoming CEO, whereas the lateral move may not seem as exciting in the short term but has a 20% probability of becoming CEO. And if they were to consider the CFO option, that would increase their eventual probability to 25%. It is simplistic when described like this and can be greatly enhanced by making more accurate estimates of compounded probabilities (that is to say, how would probabilities change if the person had been both Head of Domestic and Head of International vs Head of Domestic and CFO?). Nevertheless, this model already is a vast improvement over making career decisions with no data to guide them.

Fig. 10.4 will help to illustrate these ideas further.

The example describes the decision that an HR undergraduate is faced with upon entering the workforce after graduation, with the ultimate goal of becoming the HR VP in Asia for a large multinational firm. Initially, they are trying to decide if their first job should be as an HR generalist (business partner), a specialist

First Decision	1 Role	2 Role	Profile	Success rate for VP-HR Asia	Pre-CHRO role	Success rate for CHRO	Destination Role
	Generalist 3 years	Specialist 3 years	Generalist + Specialist	25%			
Generalist	Generalist 3 years	Generalist 3 years	Generalist	20%	VP HR Asia	30%	
Specialist	Specialist 3 years	Specialist 3 years	Specialist	15%	Global TM	25%	
Consultant	Consultant 3 years	Consultant 3 years	Consultant	10%	Global Rewards	25%	CHRO
	Consultant 3 years	Generalist 3 years	Generalist + Consultant	30%	Consulting Partner	20%	

Fig. 10.4. Potential Career Path of an HR Undergraduate.

(compensation, training, recruiting) or join an HR consulting firm. They expect this first role will take three years and that at that time they will have another decision to make about the next role they are going to take.

If their first decision was to become a generalist, the available choices at that point would be to become a specialist, or to keep going as a generalist. The option of consulting is not clear at this point, as consultancies tend to place all new hires at the beginning of the development curve, which is equivalent to starting out in consulting as a first role.

If the student, prior to graduation, had an understanding of this set of probabilities, they would take into consideration that the generalist + specialist combination has a greater probability of successfully becoming the VP HR Asia than the generalist + generalist combination (25% vs 20% respectively). And that either of those are better than going into the specialist + specialist route (15% probability of success), or even the consultant + specialist route (10% probability of success). However, they might also see that the path of greater likelihood of success (30%) is the consultant + generalist path.

If the student were to cast their aspirations further, and set the end goal to be a Global Head of HR, this model of probabilistic thinking would have led them to the VP HR Asia role as the interim step to get there, as it has a 30% chance of success, in comparison to becoming a Global HR Specialist (25% opportunity of success) or an HR Consulting Partner (20% probability of success). Following this approach can help them in making decisions about their first (and subsequent) roles.

Of course, the student may be oblivious to any of this, and only be focused on making this decision because 'that's the one with the best company name and title for my CV', or 'that's the job with the biggest pay package', etc. Thinking of only the first decision, without thinking of the combination of the next decisions, and how they combine to affect probabilities of success, may work against them in the long run. Knowing what the expected payoff in terms of careers is and understanding how the probabilities work at each step of the ladder, will help the student/employee/executive to take action in the right direction.

The reader may by now be thinking about what can be done to change the probabilities in their favour. In the case of the food stall owner, he can think about changing demand by changing the price to 90 cents or to $1.10 per bun and determine how much will demand change. He can then re-run his scenarios to decide if it is worth changing the price, and his order quantity, given his profit payoff motive.

In the case of careers, what can the incumbent do to change probabilities? Perhaps choose a good boss instead of a good company name? Or be concerned less with job title and pay and more with job skills and industry? Further their studies? Take lateral moves? Overseas assignments? Knowing what the end game is, assessing probabilities at each step, and looking into the effect of combinations of career steps into (at least a portion of) a career path can help in making decisions that benefit the company and the employee.

CASELET

In Singapore, the ICT sector wants to find way to create career paths across the various technical job families as a mean to make the sector more future-ready. They start with seven job families (see Fig. 10.5). The approach to date had been to have a career path within each job family. Each job within the job family has a job description describing what the job is meant to do and, more

SOFTWARE & APPS	SECURITY	DATA	INFRASTRUCTURE	...	...
App design and development	Governance and compliance	Data engineering	Planning and design	...	...
Systems analysis	Penetration testing	Business intelligence	Cloud computing		
Software quality assurance	Security operations	Data science	Operations and maintenance		
Platform engineering	Security intelligence and forensic				
UI/UX	Security design and engineering				
Product management					

Fig. 10.5. Job Families as Input to Career Pathing.

importantly, what skills are required to be proficient in that job. From an HR analytics point of view, the data available to prepare cross-job-family career paths consists of two pieces of information: the jobs themselves and the skills required to do each job.

With these two pieces of information, they wanted to answer the following question: For any incumbent of any job, what could be their next potential job? This information was used to map all the jobs and the skills needed to perform each job and began to look for overlaps. By comparing the skills – and the level of proficiency in the skill – that are required to do well any two jobs, if the over-lapping skills were sufficient enough, then there could be a potential career path.

The next question to answer was what constitutes an appro-priate overlap between the skills required between the jobs to make it a potential career path? They found that the answer was not straightforward. Some employees may want a bit of a stretch and would look to learn a lot more in the new job. For them a 75% overlap may not be attractive enough; they may not feel 'pushed'. For other employees, a 75% overlap may be fine: some new exposure, sufficient stretch in having to learn a quarter of the job from scratch. There was no single right answer. In either case, what mattered was having the right supporting environment for people to pick up the new skills and at the right level of proficiency for per-forming adequately at the new role. In short, the overlaps in jobs that matched skills plus proficiency levels.

The analysis ended up with just over 100 jobs to compare. At one level, this is simple: it is just comparing skill overlaps, so all that is needed is to calculate a percentage. However, there are a great many job pairs in 100+ jobs. To make this task easier, the orga-nisation went on to bundle jobs by grouping those that were adjacent, very similar.

Fig. 10.6 illustrates this point. Each individual job bundle has a set of required competencies. By comparing the amount of overlap of each job pair, it is possible to calculate the overlaps in skills. In doing this analysis it was apparent that there were several career paths available of which were unconventional. The data said: 'there's good overlap in these jobs and therefore they should be potential career paths'. And yet, how was it that no one had noticed

Job	Skills
Job A	< Skill 1, Skill 2, Skill 3, Skill 4, Skill 5, Skill 6 >
Job B	< Skill 1, Skill 3, Skill 4, Skill 6, Skill 7, Skill 8 >
Job C	< Skill 1, Skill 2, Skill 3, Skill 10, Skill 11, Skill 12 >

Feeder	Destination	Skills Overlap
Job A	Job B	= 3/6 = 50%
Job B	Job C	= 2/6 = 33%
Job C	Job A	= 3/6 = 50%

Fig. 10.6. An Example of Skills Matching for Career Planning.

these options before? The HR analytics team took these pairings that seemed unconventional back to the front-line industry leaders to confirm if these career paths made sense. The insights gained through this analysis were very powerful and allowed the team to forge new career options that did not exist before. The team ended with more than 440 career paths mapped out. Many of them were vertical moves. Nearly 120 of these were lateral moves where the overlaps were greater than 50%, and thus more viable as career paths. Fig. 10.7 shows the results of this analysis.

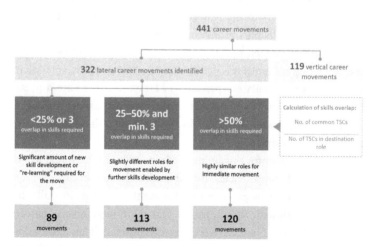

Fig. 10.7. Career Movements Identified and Corresponding Skills Overlap.

The final outcome of this work was that the long-held idea that every job movement had to involve a grade change for the individual was debunked. By starting with the proposition that both vertical and lateral moves can lead to positive career outcomes, by simplifying the analysis to consider skills overlap as a key criterion, and by getting front-line managers to agree that even unusual job movements were viable, the HR analytics team changed the way career development was done. By matching technical and soft skills to job movements, and eventually adding market/geographic knowledge as an additional criterion for senior-level promotions, they made the whole process simpler to understand and manage.

Fig. 10.8 shows an example of how skills overlaps facilitate lateral movements. In this case, a Forensic Investigation Manager is looking to transition laterally into a Senior IT Consultant role. As a first step there is the analysis of skills overlaps. These are then assessed against two additional criteria: special conditions (in this case, knowledge of the market and products) and attributes of the individual (e.g. past performance and managerial assessment results). In this manner, HR, line managers and the incumbent all can contribute to the success of this transition and align the individual for potential senior roles.

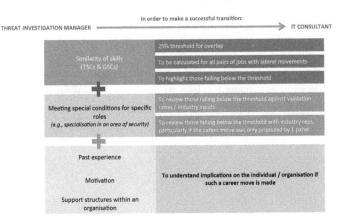

Fig. 10.8. How Skills Overlaps Facilitate Lateral Movements.

SUMMARY

In this chapter we covered an overview of decision trees, and a case example of using analytics for career pathing. Decision trees are an excellent tool to assess how different career paths can lead to different outcomes in the long run, and also how each decision along a career influences potential next steps, while precluding other options.

In the chapter we show how analytics can help to craft career paths. From the point of view of the individual, looking at each decision as a node with a probability of success towards a future goal provides insights into which direction to take, and how to chart a development path to get there. Companies can work with individuals to identify both realistic opportunities and training needs.

From the point of view of organisations, the matching of competencies to devise viable career paths also provides a means to develop individuals and retain them by providing ample and challenging learning opportunities.

QUESTIONS

1. Prepare a payoff table for the buns example described in Section 10.2.3. using opportunity cost as the decision criteria.

2. Which decisions would you have made under each of the three strategies if you did not know the probabilities?

3. When applying the probabilities to the opportunity cost, does a decision rule using EV lead to the same conclusion if you had used profit instead in the payoff table?

11

HR POLICIES VS PROFITS

In this chapter we will do a recap of multiple regression, picking up where we left off in Chapter 5, as a useful tool to determine the impact of HR policies on business results, and specifically on various metrics that can be used to measure this impact. We will also look at a couple of cases to showcase these points.

11.1 GENERAL CONCEPT OF MULTIPLE REGRESSION

Multiple regressions can be understood as an extension of simple linear regressions. We want to predict the value of a variable (called the dependent variable) based on the value of not just one but two or more independent (explanatory) variables. Let us explain these concepts through a couple of examples.

In Fig. 11.1 the employee's time with the company accounts for 15% of their compensation. Adding an additional variable to the study improves the understanding of why people earn the income they do from 22% to 37%. Using two variables, rather than one, improved our ability to make predictions about employees' salaries.

In the example in Fig. 11.2, this became more complicated; 10% of the employee's compensation is related to level 33% is related to his/her bachelor's degree and 18% is related to an interaction between level and bachelor's degree. We have increased our ability to predict employee compensation to 61%!

With this understanding in hand, let us now dig into HR metrics.

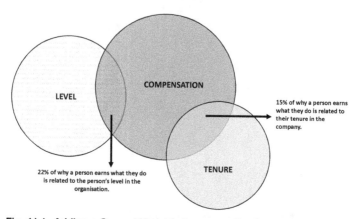

Fig. 11.1. Adding a Second Variable Increases Our Predictive Ability.

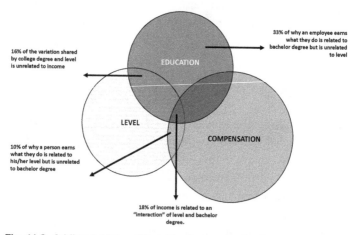

Fig. 11.2. Adding Additional Variables Increases Our Predictive Ability Further.

11.2 DEVELOP MEANINGFUL METRICS TO TRACK TALENT STRATEGY SUCCESS

There is – or at least there should be – a clear linkage between HR metrics, talent metrics and business outcomes (see Fig. 11.3). A clear linkage between HR metrics and business outcomes facilitates strategic human capital decisions and investments.

Starting from the left, the HR metrics focus on delivery of HR programs. HR metrics measure the effectiveness of the HR function

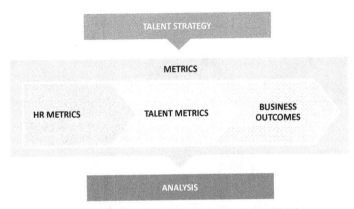

Fig. 11.3. Linkages between HR Metrics and Business Metrics.

in delivering value to enable the workforce. As such, they are fully owned by the HR department. The main concern here is to ascertain which HR activities would best support the strategies articulated in the People/Talent Strategy. In other words, if we are to build vs buy talent, for example, which are the right HR programs to do so and are they working? Are we recruiting from the right sources? Are we training people enough? And so on.

The HR metrics drive then the talent metrics. Talent metrics measure the state of workforce effectiveness in bringing about desired business outcomes. Usually, these are co-owned between HR and the business line. These are more outcome-focused inasmuch as these should describe the workforce that results from a successfully executed people strategy. Are 80% of our job openings (above entry level) filled with people promoted from within? Is our sales force at least as productive as that of our competitors? Along these lines.

Talent metrics, in turn, drive business outcomes. Business outcomes are measures of business success, fully owned by the business units. Metrics at this level are concerned with answering the question: 'How do we know if we have been successful in executing the people strategy?' For instance, Is the productivity of our sales force increasing? Would it be more profitable to add more part-time employees? Metrics at this level link HR policies with business outcomes.

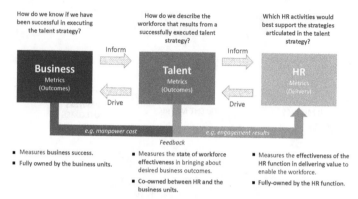

Fig. 11.4. Example of the Interaction between HR, Talent and Business Metrics.

Of course, business results will inform talent strategies, and these in turn will inform HR policies, thus closing the feedback loop. This feedback mechanism is extensive to two critical metrics in HR: manpower costs (particularly between people strategy and business outcomes) and employee engagement results (specially between talent metrics and HR metrics.

Fig. 11.4 illustrates an example of the interaction between HR, talent and business metrics. Note that each metric is measured separately and yet, they all interact in a way that each feeds others and is informed by the others.

11.3 GROCERCO CASE STUDY: CREATING AN EMPLOYEE VALUE PROPOSITION

This supermarket chain was in the midst of developing a customer value proposition to differentiate itself from its competitors. Their stated business strategy was to attract and retain customers by delivering high service value through a 'pleasant shopping experience'. By this they meant having a clean environment, easy-to-find items and efficient checkout. From an HR point of view, the challenge was to create a corresponding employment value proposition (EVP) to support the customer-centric strategy, ensuring the company was able to compete successfully and grow profitably.

To roll out the EVP, the HR team wanted to find the answer to a key question: What is the potential impact of a targeted EVP on the business and its customers? (In other words, what is the business case for implementing an EVP?) Furthermore, what are the gaps between the existing and future state and how can they be addressed?

The HR analytics team went to work using a multifaceted approach, including an empirically based assessment of the drivers of workforce outcomes and business performance – combined with stakeholder interviews and surveys, focus groups, recruiter interviews and exit interviews. From their initial analyses, the work quickly revolved around three main hypotheses, and the company created project teams to drive change in these areas:

- Talent acquisition/onboarding (e.g. integration of new hires),

- Total rewards (e.g. financial rewards and performance management),

- Work design and processes (e.g. work scheduling).

One initial finding related to the causes of voluntary turnover, based on the premise that 'voting with their feet' was an important summary indicator of how the EVP was viewed by employees. The results of this analysis are shown in Fig. 11.5.

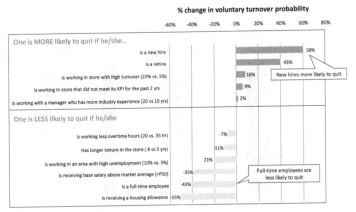

Fig. 11.5. % Change in Voluntary Turnover Probability.

Note that, in this case, new hires and rehires are more likely to quit, and that full-time employees are less likely to quit. These results led to further analysis along these lines. Fig. 11.6 shows the results of one of the 'quick quits' analyses. The numbers show that almost two out of every five new hires quit within their first year of employment. These results indicate problems in the recruiting of new staff.

A second key hypothesis of the EVP related to what the organisation was (and was not) rewarding. The HR analytics team defined 'rewards' as the likelihood that the employee would have base pay growth and the likelihood that an employee would be promoted. They plotted these two variables in a 2 × 2 matrix – which was built using historical data – regarding the probability that a particular employee characteristic was correlated with pay increases or promotions. The results are summarised in Fig. 11.7. Note that, for instance, rehires are paid more but are less likely to receive a promotion or pay raise. Similarly, employees with college education are more likely to receive both a promotion and pay increases, which is indicative of a pay-for-performance link. This analysis helped the company understand which groups of employees are more likely to stay (or to leave!).

The third hypothesis is related to the impact that work scheduling (and other elements of the EVP) had on store profitability. Their results are summarised in Fig. 11.8. Note that stores with more rehired employees had lower monthly profits, whereas stores

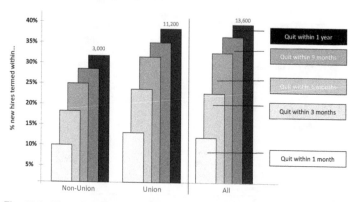

Fig. 11.6. New Hire 'Quick Quits' for Employees by Union Affiliation.

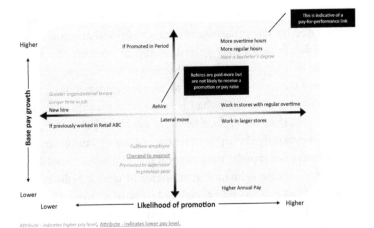

Fig. 11.7. Factors Affecting the Probability of Promotion or Increased Pay.

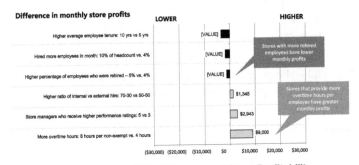

Fig. 11.8. Elements of the EVP Which Impact Store Profitability.

with more overtime per employee had greater monthly profits. It is also important to note that longer tenured employees were correlated with smaller monthly profits. These two groups of employees (rehired and longer-tenured) likely represent a higher cost to the company and yet, they do not contribute to store profitability. This represented a dilemma for the HR function, which up until that point was rallying for rehires and longer tenure as 'good for morale', not knowing that these groups of employees in fact had a negative impact on the business.

As a result of this analysis, the team wanted to investigate further if indeed it was true that increasing (versus decreasing, which is what they expected) overtime hours would improve monthly profits. Fig. 11.9 shows the results of this additional analysis, which provided details on the least desired number of overtime hours, and how these two variables, overtime hours and monthly profits, were related in what to the HR team was a counterintuitive way. Store managers up until that point had been asked to minimise overtime. It turned out that, up to four hours of overtime per month, was true. But beyond five hours of overtime per month (and at least up to nine hours per month) store profitability actually increased.

Another area the team looked at related to work scheduling was the mix of full-time to part-time employees in a store. The store managers had been of the belief that part-time workers were more profitable as they received lower benefits. However, that was only true up to a point: The results are illustrated in Fig. 11.9, which shows that the benefits of reducing the percentage of full-time staff begins to drop off below 38% (Fig. 11.10).

At the end of their multiple streams of analyses (and note that several of these were done using multiple regressions), the team identified five primary levers for creating GrocerCo's EVP. Fig. 11.11 shows these, including the three hypotheses they had started out with, plus two more that were discovered along the way. The latter were related to the development of internal talent and to diversity and inclusion.

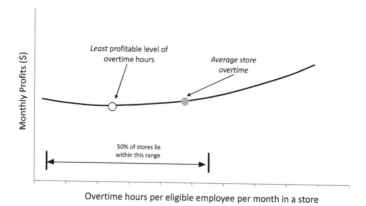

Fig. 11.9. Overtime Hours per Eligible Employee per Month in a Store.

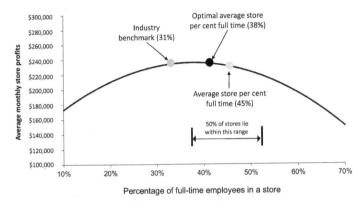

Fig. 11.10. Percentage of Full-time Employees in a Store.

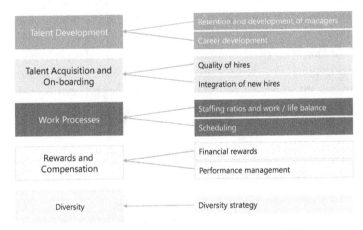

Fig. 11.11. Five Primary Levers for Creating GrocerCo's EVP.

This analytic work identified several opportunities to increase average annual gross profit while at the same time improving the EVP of the company, thus making it easier to attract and retain talent. In addition, they did learn quite a number of things along the way. They did a better job of rehiring and onboarding, they changed the way they paid employees, they focused training and rewards metrics on customer satisfaction, they put in variable pay store-wide and department-wide but they did not base individual pay on customer satisfaction. They also did not measure customer satisfaction by department, but rather by store. They did lose about

20% of their people in that year, but the EVP proved to be very successful (work scheduling alone yielded additional profits of $8 million). To this day, GrocerCo is still quite profitable.

11.4 RETAILCO CASE STUDY: USING ANALYTICS TO IMPROVE RETENTION AND STORE SALES

A shoe retail chain recognised that the company's store model could be easily copied, and thus wanted to find ways to increase their competitive advantage. They were concerned that if competitors could successfully copy their business model, it would affect the firm's financial performance. Competition was expected to intensify as the company prepared to enter more markets and build more stores.

Among other strategic decisions, RetailCo wanted to understand and optimise the 'people' drivers of store performance, so they could come up with a people management approach that competitors could not easily copy. In this case, they were looking to answer the following business questions:

- With many people programs in place: how can they tell which practices really influence sales?

- How can the company achieve the optimal staffing mix, training level and supervision to maximise sales and reduce employee costs?

The HR analytics team wanted to measure the direct impact of various people practices on store performance and retention, after controlling for different factors such as seasonality, location, inventory and staffing. By fine-tuning existing staffing practices, their hypothesis was that the company could increase gross sales (and resulting profit) by over 5%.

The statistical analyses focused on three broad categories of drivers that had an impact on both employee turnover and sales volume: external influences, store attributes and individual attributes. The breakdown of the data analysed within each category was as follows:

- External Influences
  - Local unemployment rates
  - Distance to work
  - Local labour pool (diversity, education, age, income)
  - Organisational Practices
- Store attributes
  - Size
  - Spans of control
  - Promotion rates
  - Turnover rates
  - Age
  - Tenure
  - Diversity
  - Prior year's sales trends
  - Supervisor promotion rates, turnover rates, age, tenure
  - Non-supervisor promotion rates, turnover rates, age, tenure
- Individual attributes
  - Age
  - Gender
  - Ethnicity
  - Tenure
  - Performance ratings
  - Compensation (base, variable)
  - Job status (full vs part-time)
  - Participation in training
  - Internal mobility (promotions, career-level changes)
  - Employment status (active, terminated, on leave)

- Hire source (new hire, rehire)

- Location (work, home)

The analyses uncovered that many factors played a role in retention of employees, including pay, overtime and training. Fig. 11.12 shows the percentage change in voluntary turnover probability. The results show that employees who receive overtime are less likely to leave; in fact, an increase in overtime hours from 0 to 10 hours per month reduced the likelihood that a person would leave the company by more than 60%.

The team also wanted to ascertain how much did external and internal factors influence sales. They found both factors that increased and that decreased store sales (see Fig. 11.13), and were also able to determine, via multiple regressions, which factors had greater weight. For instance, having many new hires in the store had the greatest positive effect on sales. On the other hand, having too many full-time employees was detrimental to store sales.

Armed with this new knowledge, instead of 'hoping for the best', the company applied store-specific performance enhancers to reduce waste in staffing and improve sales, opening up funds to hire people with critical competencies, and encouraging the development of strong store managers. Store sales did increase 5% overall.

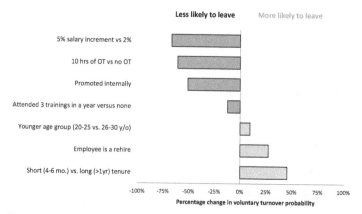

Fig. 11.12. Percentage Change in Voluntary Turnover Probability.

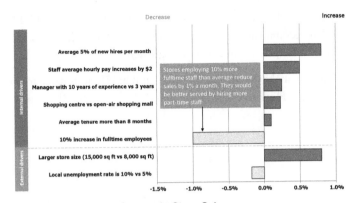

Fig. 11.13. Percentage Change in Store Sales.

SUMMARY

In this chapter we have covered basic elements of multiple regressions as well as what metrics to use to measure the impact of HR on business results.

We then put these concepts to use in delving into two case studies, which show how HR analytics can inform business decisions and drive business outcomes. By measuring how HR policies impact revenue growth and profitability, the HR analytics team was able to add value both to the business and to the HR function.

QUESTIONS

1. When does it make sense to use multiple regressions? Or is it enough to do a series of single regressions addressing each of the variables of interest?

2. Can you distinguish between HR metrics and talent metrics? When should each of these be used?

3. In the case of GrocerCo, how would you measure the success of the EVP initiative? What other analyses would you recommend? Which recommendations would you make given the data shown?

4. What conclusions can you draw from the data on Fig. 11.13? What recommendations would you give RetailCo in terms of future HR policies to drive sales growth?

5. Can you make a convincing argument that HR adds value to the business? How would you go about it?

12

CONCLUSIONS AND THOUGHTS ON THE FUTURE OF HR ANALYTICS

12.1 DOES HR ADD VALUE?

An organisation gains a competitive advantage by developing its staff to form a unique and valuable human capital pool. Senior management often attribute the success of their organisations to good leadership supported by capable staff. However, they often also hesitate to invest in staff for fear of not realising sufficient return on investment. Human Capital Strategy poses that an organisation can gain competitive advantage from putting in place the appropriate human capital strategies and HR programs and policies to help implement the business strategy through people. Throughout this book we have endeavoured to show how these HR practices, intended to enhance employees' knowledge, skills, abilities, motivation and opportunity to contribute, are associated with positive operational and financial outcomes. We have also argued that other important effects are that employee engagement increases while voluntary turnover is significantly reduced by good HR practices.

This all seems simple and straightforward; then why is the HR profession still struggling to 'get a seat at the table' and be considered a full-fledged business partner? This book makes the case that, to be strategic, HR must focus on predicting people needs in line with business plans, solving problems that get in the way of achieving the predicted outcomes and implementing HR practices that add value to the business. It is in these three areas that we aim to make a contribution to HR practitioners.

Throughout the book we expanded on the notion that a data-driven approach to people decisions will lead to a productive organisation.

12.2 CUTTING COSTS IS LESS STRATEGIC THAN DRIVING REVENUE GROWTH

For many HR professionals, becoming involved with the financials of the company usually means focusing on ways to cut costs out of the enterprise and of reducing the cost of delivering HR services. When cost reduction efforts are implemented the results can be fairly significant in the short term. However, over time, the value of the savings is limited in accordance with the principle of diminishing returns. These cost reduction efforts are good initiatives in themselves but are more tactical in nature. To truly be strategic as a function, HR must focus on ways to help increase revenue growth and productivity.

To make this point clearer, let us assess the difference between reducing by 10% the cost of delivering HR services and the potential gain of 1% improvement in labour productivity.

A typical HR function represents approximately 4% of the corporate budget. However, HR typically manages about 60% of total company costs, which is made up of all the payroll and related workforce expenses. The HR function would add more value if it focused on improving productivity by 1% per year than trying to reduce delivery costs by 10% per year. And the long-term results would be more sustainable!

A simple example will illustrate this point.

- Assume the company has expenses of $100,000,000.

- The HR department expenses would be $4,000,000.

- The workforce expenses would be $60,000,000.

- The value of 10% reduction in HR costs would be
  10% × $4,000,000 = $400,000.

- The value of 1% gain in labour productivity would be
  1% × $60,000,000 = $600,000.

- That's a difference of 50%!

12.3 PRODUCTIVITY, REVENUE AND PROFIT IMPACT OF HR PROGRAMS

HR professionals generally 'know' that increasing employee engagement and lowering turnover is linked to better business outcomes. But, as we said in the first chapter, if HR wants to be heard, it needs to be able to put HR arguments in business language, using data to link HR decisions to business outcomes. HR analytics helps HR to demonstrate that the function positively impacts employee productivity, revenue and profit.

Throughout the book we have maintained that building hypotheses based on business problems, defining the 'Y-variable' as a business outcome, taking care of the data, applying the needed financial and statistical knowledge, looking for insights in an iterative process and telling the story succinctly and convincingly are the key elements of 'proving' that an HR program delivers results. The analysis can take various forms:

- A pilot run

- A comparison between baseline (before the program is applied) and after program implementation (say in the case of quality training; did quality improve afterwards)

- A correlation that shows how one variable goes up or down if another moves up or down (say, does a higher pay mix for the sales force lead to higher sales)

- An after-the-fact assessment (in cases where there is no baseline data)

Throughout the various chapters, we have looked at specific examples where we apply HR analytics to better understand how to drive results from various HR practice areas. In the following section, we provide some practical advice on how HR practitioners can tackle various HR issues.

12.3.1 Turnover

- Do lower performing employees stay shorter with the company? Do you have too many top performers leaving? Do you know why they are leaving? Or why are they staying?

- Are 'highly rated' (by their supervisors) managers better able to retain their employees? What makes them better? Can that be replicated in the organisation?

- Ask ex-employees (three to six months after termination) the 'real' reason why they left the organisation to determine the factors that need to be addressed to reduce turnover.

12.3.2 Training

- Determine the number of hours of sales training needed to impact sales results. What is the shape of the relationship? Does it vary by product line? Geography? Tenure? Past performance? Calculate the increased revenue and profits vs the cost of training to build a business case.

- Equally, show the correlation between the number of hours a manufacturing or support employee receives in training and the resulting productivity, error rates, accidents and product quality. Calculate the savings from the reduced errors and accidents, and the added quality, to determine the ROI of the training.

12.3.3 Workforce Planning

- Determine the cost of building vs buying talent; compare it to the organisation's ability to meet the growth needs of the business by finding/promoting the right. Where should the company invest more? In hiring or in training?

- Add to the above the cost of moving an expat vs the cost of hiring locals (could be more than one!) and the expected results of each decision. Is it justified to bring expats?

12.3.4 Recruiting

- Compare the cost and output of newly hired employees to the cost and output of newly promoted employees for the same role. Is it more productive to recruit from the outside? Or to promote from within?

- Run a pilot employee referral program in one location and determine if there is an increase in quality of hires and a reduction in cost and time to hire.

- Ask new hires why they accepted the job with the company and create a ranking from the reasons given; employee value proposition, company reputation, quality of leadership, etc.

12.3.5 Compensation

- Determine if an increase in the amount of performance bonus increases performance.

- Show that giving a worker a 10% bonus for a specific outcome (say, customer satisfaction) improves results by more than 10%. Calculate the ROI.

- Validate if team incentives yield better business outcomes than individual incentives.

- Calculate the productivity improvement trend (revenue or profit divided by total workforce cost). Is it improving year on year? How does it compare to competitors'?

12.3.6 Career Planning

- Calculate the retention rate of high-potential employees whose career the company has been managing closely. Is it better than for other employee groups?

- Estimate the probabilities that a certain career path will yield the desired development opportunities both for the employees and for the company.

12.3.7 HR Policies

- Determine how the various HR programs contribute to the metrics that the Board of Directors/CEO expects the business to achieve. Calculate the ROI of each program (or combinations of programs).

- Learn to translate HR metrics into financial/business metrics. And continue to teach other business leaders about the value HR brings by showing them evidence of instances where HR has helped to grow revenue and profits (and not only improve engagement and reduce turnover).

12.4 WHAT'S NEXT?

In the near future, the HR function will be delivered very differently than it is today, given the impact that digitalisation, artificial intelligence and robotics is having on the workforce and on the HR profession.

As the HR function evolves, HR practitioners will need to add to their skills and capabilities. A 2018 survey by David Green and Ian Bailie at myHRfuture identified key skills HR professionals need to develop, in order of their future importance:

- People Analytics

- Digital HR/HR Technologies

- Change Management

- Consulting and Influencing

- Agile Working

- Strategic Workforce Planning

- Ethics and Data Privacy

- Design Thinking

- Stakeholder Management

- Diversity and Inclusion

- AI, Robotics and Future of Work

- Employer Branding

'People analytics' came in at the most important in the survey, along with 'digital HR/HR technologies.' And yet, the next two were 'soft' skills like change management and consulting/ influencing. It is clear that HR professionals need to become more analytical, but it is equally clear that the profession needs to also stay grounded on its human aspects.

In line with these results, we believe all HR professionals must be conversant in HR analytics, if the function is to be effective at improving individual performance, enhancing employee experience and helping to achieve business goals. HR professionals tradition- ally have shied away from gaining basic data literacy skills, including data visualisation, finance and statistics. It is our hope that more HR practitioners will see the need to become more analytical if they wish to keep pace with the new demands on the profession and be an integral part of a more data-driven, yet human-grounded, future of the HR profession.

12.4.1 A Glimpse of the HR Future?

There are analytics capabilities built into most new and upcoming software offerings, which has increased our ability to collect and analyse data that, until recently, was not available. The availability of these data holds the promise that they can help HR analytics teams understand how they can improve the employee experience.

Real-time sentiment and emotion recognition analysis is a fast-growing field, which is increasingly being used to measure how employees are feeling. There is already technology available which can analyse a person's facial nano-expressions and gauge their current emotion, such as happiness, anger or sadness. It can also predict if the person is truthful or surprised. Similar technology for voice analysis is already available to assess feelings from voice patterns.

Biosensors and wearables are widely available for personal health and fitness, providing data for physiological metrics (heart rate, sleep patterns, blood pressure, etc.), as well as various environmental metrics (distance, altitude, etc.). Similar devices are used in the workplace to help improve health and safety – for example, devices can be worn by truck drivers to alert them if they are falling asleep while driving. Other devices are being used in high volume work settings to help improve productivity by alerting employees when they are not focused or when their stress levels are too high.

However, future applications do not need to always be so individualised. Improving any HR process (take on-line training, for example) is a good opportunity to apply a design-thinking mindset, get feedback from users, supervisors, vendors and other stakeholders, use the feedback to re-design the process, pilot the new approach and collect data to see if they are more effective and efficient than the old process. Is it cheaper/faster/better and does it help to increase productivity/revenues/profits? Does it make the employee experience better?

Many questions still remain about this ability to track and use data. We need to overcome the lack of skills to analyse the data. Technology, and the resulting data, must be validated, especially when it comes to interpreting feelings and thoughts. The new technologies have access to sensitive areas, raising concerns about data storage and usage, and there may be some who want to hoard or misuse these data, which will lead to regulation at some point on how it can be used and interpreted. Personal data protection legislation is already in place in many jurisdictions and will likely continue to evolve rapidly as technologies become more powerful and available. There will also be many, both HR professionals and employees, who will resist change. The handling of sensitive information on an employee's health or feelings must be handled with extreme care. The HR function and the analytics team will need to continuously monitor and update their policies and procedures – and communicate these to employees – about what type of data are being collected, for what purpose, for how long, where they are stored and the data protection mechanisms in place.

Whatever the future holds, it is an exciting time to be an HR professional.

REFERENCES

Boudreau, J. W. (2010). *Retooling HR*. Boston, MA: Harvard Business School Publishing.

Bussin, M., & Diez, F. (2016). *The remuneration handbook* (International ed.). Johannesburg: Knowledge Resources Private Limited.

Diez, F. (2018). Pay for performance: What type of pay scheme is best for achieving business results? Lambert Academic Publishing.

Evans, J. R. (2017). *Business analytics* (2nd ed.). London: Pearson.

Forman, D. C. (2007). *The talent scorecard: Practical people analytics across the talent lifecycle*. White paper. Human Capital Institute, New York, NY.

Guenole, N., Ferrar, J., & Feinzig, S. (2017). *The power of people: Learn how successful organisations use workforce analytics to improve business performance*. New York, NY: Pearson FT Press.

Nalbantian, H., Guzzo, R., Kieffer, D., & Doherty, J. (2003). *Play to your strengths: Managing your internal labour markets for lasting competitive advantage*. New York, NY: McGraw-Hill Education.

Pease, G., Byerly, B., & Fitz-enz, J. (2013). *Human capital analytics*. Hoboken, NJ: John Wiley & Sons.

Phillips, P. P., & Phillips, J. J. (2015). *Making human capital analytics work: Measuring the ROI of human capital process and outcomes*. New York, NY: McGraw-Hill Education.

Provost, F., & Fawcett, T. (2013). *Data science for business*. Sebastopol, CA: O'Reilly Media Inc.

Thomas, H., Smith, R., & Diez, F. (2013). *Human capital and global business strategies*. New York, NY: Cambridge University Press.

INDEX

Printed in the USA
CPSIA information can be obtained
at www.ICGtesting.com
LVHW050324150923
758166LV00005B/345